Building your First Mobile Game using XNA 4.0

A fast-paced, hands-on guide to building a 3D game for the Windows Phone 7 platform using XNA 4.0

Brecht Kets

Thomas Goussaert

[PACKT] enterprise
PUBLISHING
professional expertise distilled

BIRMINGHAM - MUMBAI

Building your First Mobile Game using XNA 4.0

First published: December 2012

Production Reference: 1191212

Published by Packt Publishing Ltd.
Livery Place
35 Livery Street
Birmingham B3 2PB, UK.

ISBN 978-1-84968-774-4

www.packtpub.com

Cover Image by Lino Drieghe (contact@linodriegheart.com)

Credits

Authors
Brecht Kets

Thomas Goussaert

Reviewers
Kurt Jaegers

Justin Witol

Cătălin Zima-Zegreanu

Acquisition Editor
Dilip Venkatesh

Commissioning Editor
Meeta Rajani

Technical Editors
Kaustubh S. Mayekar

Kirti Pujari

Project Coordinator
Michelle Quadros

Proofreader
Mario Cecere

Indexer
Hemangini Bari

Graphics
Aditi Gajjar

Production Coordinator
Melwyn D'sa

Cover Work
Melwyn D'sa

About the Authors

Brecht Kets is a Senior Lecturer at Howest University in Belgium, where he teaches game development in one of the leading international game development study programs, Digital Arts and Entertainment (www.digitalartsandentertainment. com). He's been actively involved in game development for several years, and has been writing about XNA since the launch in December 2006. He hosts the website www.3dgameprogramming.net and has received the Microsoft Most Valuable Professional award in the category DirectX/XNA five times in a row for his contributions in the community.

Brecht has also co-authored the video series *XNA 3D Game Development By Example, Packt Publishing*.

Thomas Goussaert graduated in Digital Arts And Entertainment (DAE), from Howest University. With a wide range of skills acquired by his studies, he explored the world of programming and game development. Thomas is always curious and eager to learn new things; always feeding his passion for programming. Now he's a lecturer at Howest University, where he teaches game development in one of the leading international game development study programs, Digital Arts and Entertainment (www.digitalartsandentertainment.com). It's nice to have a passion for programming, but it's even better to share it with the world!

Thomas has also co-authored the video series XNA 3D Game Development By Example, Packt Publishing

Acknowledgement

First of all, we would like to thank our family and friends for supporting us while writing this book, without which this series would not have been possible. We would also like to thank everyone at Packt Publishing for giving us this opportunity, along with the reviewers who did an excellent job at making this book what it is.

Finally we would like to thank Mike Ptacek for providing us with the artwork for this series, making coder-art needless and sparing your eyes from permanent damage. We would also like to thank Lino Drieghe for making the cover image of this book.

About the Reviewers

Kurt Jaegers is an Oracle Database Administrator and Windows network Admin, as well as a long-time hobbyist game developer. He has built games for everything from the Commodore 64 to the Xbox 360. He is the owner of http://www.xnaresources.com, and the author of *XNA Game Development by Example*, *Packt Publishing* for both C# and Visual Basic, and *XNA 4 3D Game Development by Example*, *Packt Publishing*.

Justin Witol grew up programming and he loved it ever since he was young when his mother first introduced him to Basic. For the past few years he has been working on game programming and has been developing an open source game engine for practice. He helps out within the community mainly dealing with C# and XNA, but at times he helps out in other fields as well, so when asked about reviewing this book he immediately responded with a yes. He hopes the book has helped to further your understanding of not only game development but programming in general. If you ever have any questions or just need some help with something dealing with programming feel free to stop by his website at www.WitolProductions.com and just ask.

Cătălin Zima-Zegreanu is very passionate about game design and development. He has been working with games and graphics technologies for more than the last seven years. He has been awarded the title of Microsoft MVP for DirectX/XNA for five years, in recognition of his expertise and dedication to the technology. At the moment, he is designing and developing mobile games with an awesome team, and enjoying life with awesome family and friends.

www.PacktPub.com

Support files, eBooks, discount offers and more

You might want to visit www.PacktPub.com for support files and downloads related to your book.

Did you know that Packt offers eBook versions of every book published, with PDF and ePub files available? You can upgrade to the eBook version at www.PacktPub.com and as a print book customer, you are entitled to a discount on the eBook copy. Get in touch with us at service@packtpub.com for more details.

At www.PacktPub.com, you can also read a collection of free technical articles, sign up for a range of free newsletters and receive exclusive discounts and offers on Packt books and eBooks.

http://PacktLib.PacktPub.com

Do you need instant solutions to your IT questions? PacktLib is Packt's online digital book library. Here, you can access, read and search across Packt's entire library of books.

Why Subscribe?

- Fully searchable across every book published by Packt
- Copy and paste, print and bookmark content
- On demand and accessible via web browser

Free Access for Packt account holders

If you have an account with Packt at www.PacktPub.com, you can use this to access PacktLib today and view nine entirely free books. Simply use your login credentials for immediate access.

Instant Updates on New Packt Books

Get notified! Find out when new books are published by following @PacktEnterprise on Twitter, or the *Packt Enterprise* Facebook page.

Table of Contents

Preface

Welcome to the world of mobile game development. By purchasing this book, you've made the first step towards building your first game for the Windows Phone platform.

In this book, we will first go over the technical stuff, like installing the tools, drawing 2D and 3D images, and end up building a 3D game for Windows Phone 7 together! Let's get started!

What this book covers

Chapter 1, Getting Started, is an introductory chapter where we define how we can build games for Windows Phone, install the necessary tools, and create our first project.

Chapter 2, 2D Graphics, covers drawing 2D images to the screen, moving them, and playing animations. We will also start creating a basic framework for our future game here.

Chapter 3, 3D Graphics, gives us more information about drawing 3D models, along with playing animations. The chapter also covers the concept of World, View, and Projection, and the concept of a camera.

Chapter 4, Input, will help us to add player interaction to our game, covering touch input, keyboard, and the accelerometer.

Chapter 5, Sound, will help us set the mood for our game. In this chapter, we will learn how to play sounds and apply effects to them, play 3D sound, and play songs.

Chapter 6, Building a Basic Framework, teaches us how to finalize our framework, so we are ready for building our game. This chapter introduces the concepts of a scene graph, a scene manager, and collision detection. It also shows us how to build menus.

Chapter 7, Building a Game, is the chapter where we build a game from scratch!

Chapter 8, Releasing our Game, gives us information on what to do after we finish our game. It gives information on how to release the game to the Windows Phone Marketplace and the certification process.

What you need for this book

Beside a healthy interest in building games, this book expects that you have knowledge about C# and some basic knowledge about math. Besides that, the book explains everything from the ground up.

You also need a computer with Windows Vista or newer (all editions except Starter Edition), 4 GB of free disk space, 3 GB RAM, and a DirectX10 or above capable graphics card.

Who this book is for

In this mini book, we won't have time to cover everything, so we assume you already have some experience with object-oriented programming. This book will cover the basics of building a game for Windows Phone, but we won't explain the C# programming language itself, nor object-oriented programming.

We will however explain the aspects of game development thoroughly, so don't worry if you have never written a (3D) game. We will cover all the basics here, including the much dreaded math. However, don't expect to write triple-A games, when you've finished this book, but you'll be off in the world of indie game development.

This is the right book for anyone, regardless of age and gender, if:

- You are interested in game development
- You want to start building games for Windows Phone
- You have some programming knowledge

Conventions

In this book, you will find a number of styles of text that distinguish between different kinds of information. Here are some examples of these styles, and an explanation of their meaning.

Code words in text are shown as follows: "We can include other contexts through the use of the `include` directive."

A block of code is set as follows:

```
public class RenderContext
{
    public SpriteBatch SpriteBatch { get; set; }
    public GraphicsDevice GraphicsDevice { get; set; }
    public GameTime GameTime { get; set; }
}
```

New terms and **important words** are shown in bold. Words that you see on the screen, in menus or dialog boxes for example, appear in the text like this: "clicking the **Next** button moves you to the next screen".

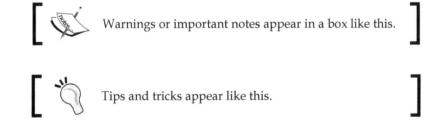

Warnings or important notes appear in a box like this.

Tips and tricks appear like this.

Reader feedback

Feedback from our readers is always welcome. Let us know what you think about this book—what you liked or may have disliked. Reader feedback is important for us to develop titles that you really get the most out of.

To send us general feedback, simply send an e-mail to `feedback@packtpub.com`, and mention the book title through the subject of your message.

If there is a topic that you have expertise in and you are interested in either writing or contributing to a book, see our author guide on `www.packtpub.com/authors`.

Customer support

Now that you are the proud owner of a Packt book, we have a number of things to help you to get the most from your purchase.

Downloading the example code

You can download the example code files for all Packt books you have purchased from your account at http://www.packtpub.com. If you purchased this book elsewhere, you can visit http://www.packtpub.com/support and register to have the files e-mailed directly to you.

Downloading the color images of this book

We also provide you a PDF file that has color images of the screenshots/diagrams used in this book. The color images will help you better understand the changes in the output.

You can download this file from http://www.packtpub.com/sites/default/files/downloads/7744EN_ColoredImages.pdf.

Errata

Although we have taken every care to ensure the accuracy of our content, mistakes do happen. If you find a mistake in one of our books—maybe a mistake in the text or the code—we would be grateful if you would report this to us. By doing so, you can save other readers from frustration and help us improve subsequent versions of this book. If you find any errata, please report them by visiting http://www.packtpub.com/support, selecting your book, clicking on the **errata submission form** link, and entering the details of your errata. Once your errata are verified, your submission will be accepted and the errata will be uploaded to our website, or added to any list of existing errata, under the Errata section of that title.

Piracy

Piracy of copyright material on the Internet is an ongoing problem across all media. At Packt, we take the protection of our copyright and licenses very seriously. If you come across any illegal copies of our works, in any form, on the Internet, please provide us with the location address or website name immediately so that we can pursue a remedy.

Please contact us at copyright@packtpub.com with a link to the suspected pirated material.

We appreciate your help in protecting our authors, and our ability to bring you valuable content.

Questions

You can contact us at questions@packtpub.com if you are having a problem with any aspect of the book, and we will do our best to address it.

1
Getting Started

Welcome to the world of Windows Phone development. By reading this book you've made the first step necessary to write games for Windows Phone. Let's get started!

In this chapter we will cover:

- The basics of developing games for the Windows Phone platform
- Getting up and running with Windows Phone SDK
- Deploying our first app to the emulator and to a Windows Phone device
- The structure of the XNA Game class

Developing for Windows Phone

Let us start by talking about the Windows Phone platform itself. All Windows Phone devices have minimum sets of hardware they have to comply with. This includes three buttons: start, search, and back, a resolution of 480x800, a touch screen, an accelerometer, and more. The list of specifications can be found at `http://msdn.microsoft.com/en-us/library/windowsphone/develop/ff637514(v=vs.92).aspx`.

With the launch of Windows Phone 7 back in 2010, Microsoft offered two possible ways to develop applications for Windows Phone. The applications we write must be developed using either Silverlight or XNA Game Studio 4.0. Both Silverlight and XNA are powered by the .NET framework. This means we can develop apps for Windows Phone using managed programming languages such as C# (version 3). This book will only cover XNA development, as this framework is very suitable for developing games. We won't be discussing Silverlight.

But first, what is XNA? XNA is a managed framework which runs on top of the .NET framework. It enables us to build games for Windows, Xbox 360, and Windows Phone, with limited adaptations to the source code when switching to another platform. Because it runs on top of the .NET framework, you can use VB.NET or C# as programming languages. In this book, we will use C# and won't cover VB.NET.

What makes XNA interesting in terms of game development is that it takes care of the boring stuff (initializing and maintaining the graphics device and setting up your render loop for instance) for us; this enables us to skip the boiler plate code and focus on the interesting part, being our game.

XNA Game Studio 4.0 – the development environment for XNA – is part of the Windows Phone SDK. This toolset is an extension for Visual Studio 2010, and is available for free. Using XNA Game Studio 4.0, you can develop XNA games for Windows Phone (amongst others), and deploy to an emulator or an actual Windows Phone device. However, when you want to deploy to an actual device, the device has to be registered. To register your Windows Phone, you need a valid Dev Center Developer account, which costs $99 annually – unless you are a student. Students can get a free (limited) developer account through www.dreamspark.com. A valid Dev Center Developer account will enable you to create games for and deploy them to Windows Phone. This does not include deploying to Xbox 360.

Installing the Windows Phone SDK

Let us start by installing all the software we need. XNA Game Studio 4.0 (our development environment) is part of the Windows Phone SDK. You can download the latest version from https://dev.windowsphone.com/en-us/downloadsdk. At the time of writing, the most recent version is 'Windows Phone SDK 7.1'. The setup will install the following applications:

- Microsoft Visual Studio 2010 Express for Windows Phone
- Windows Phone Emulator
- Windows Phone SDK Assemblies
- Windows Phone SDK Extensions for XNA Game Studio 4.0
- Microsoft Expression Blend SDK for Windows Phone
- Silverlight 4 SDK and DRT
- WCF Data Services Client for Windows Phone
- Microsoft Advertising SDK for Windows Phone

Note that all these applications will enable you to build applications for Windows Phone 7.0 and Windows Phone 7.5. The tools we will use are the Windows Phone Emulator and XNA Game Studio 4.0.

When you already have a version of Visual Studio 2010 installed (Professional for instance), the add-ins for this version will be installed automatically. Make sure you have all service packs installed for that installation version.

After installing the SDK, make sure you install the latest update. This can be downloaded from the same location as the SDK. At the time of writing, the latest update is 'Windows Phone SDK 7.1.1 Update'.

Registering your Windows Phone

To be able to deploy games to our Windows Phone, we need to register the device. There are three prerequisites:

- Obtain a Microsoft account if you don't have one. This can be done through www.live.com.

- Create a valid Dev Center Developer account (if you don't have one). This can be done through https://dev.windowsphone.com/en-us/join. An Dev Center Developer account costs $99 annually, and it will enable you to deploy games to Windows Phone.

- If you are a student, you can register for free using a valid DreamSpark account. Go to www.dreamspark.com to register. Your university/school representative can help you out here.

- Install Zune from www.zune.net.

Once the above is taken care of, we can start registering our Windows Phone. Start by making sure that the date and time are correct and connect your phone to your PC using the USB cable. Zune will start automatically. If it does not start, we need to start it ourselves. If everything went okay, the phone will appear in the '**Device**' tab of the Zune software. On the first run, this might take a few minutes, while Windows installs the drivers for the phone.

Next we can open the Windows Phone Developer registration tool we can find by clicking **Start | All Programs | Windows Phone SDK 7.1**. Once the application has started, you should see the following window:

Once the status says **Phone ready**, register using your Microsoft account.

Getting started with your first application

Let us start by creating our first—empty—application, and deploying it to the emulator or an actual Windows Phone device.

After installing everything, go ahead and open up Microsoft Visual Studio 2010 Express for Windows Phone or your Visual Studio 2010 if you have another version installed.

1. Go to **File** | **New** | **Project**. The **New Project** window will pop up as shown in the following screenshot:

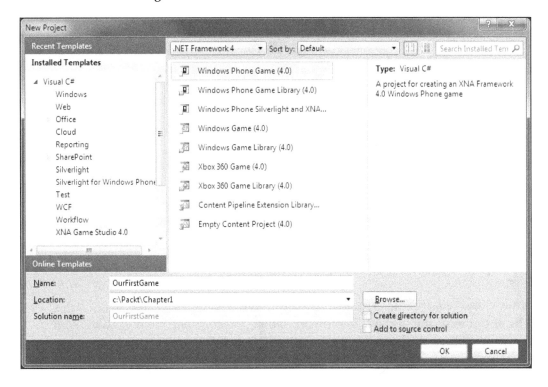

2. Among the installed templates (on the left-hand side of the **New Project** window) we can find **XNA Game Studio 4.0**. Click it and select **Windows Phone Game (4.0)** in the middle of the screen.

3. At the bottom of the window, we can give our game a proper name and choose a file location for our game. Click on the **OK** button.

4. Next we get asked which platform of Windows Phone we want to develop for, that is 7.0 or 7.1. Go ahead and choose **Windows Phone OS 7.1** as illustrated in the following screenshot and click on **OK**.

 With Windows Phone OS 7.0, Microsoft means the Windows Phone 7 Mango devices. Windows Phone OS 7.1 means the Windows Phone 7.5 Tango devices.

Now XNA Game Studio created a new project that contains a class called Game1. This is our main game class. Don't worry about the code yet, we will go over this in the next chapters. The important part is that everything is set up for us to begin.

Take a look at the toolbars at the top. There you can find a drop-down menu where we can select what device we want to deploy to.

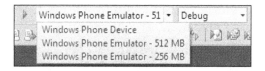

We can choose between a Windows Phone device, an emulator with 512 MB RAM, and an emulator with 256 MB RAM. The latter aims at the low end devices. Choose **Windows Phone Emulator – 512 MB**. If you want to deploy to an actual device, choose **Windows Phone Device**; make sure it is connected to your PC and that the Zune Software is running. The device also needs to be unlocked. During development, it can be wise to make sure the device doesn't lock automatically. This can be done via **Settings | Lock + Wallpaper | Screen time out after**.

When you press *F5*, our game will be compiled and then deployed. After everything is loaded correctly, two different screens pop up. With the **Additional Tools** window, we can simulate the accelerometer, GPS data, and take screenshots. On the phone emulator, we can see an empty, cornflower blue screen.

This might not seem like a lot, but our entire render loop has been made, and we are ready to start loading content and displaying models. Let's get going!

The Game class

Let's go over the Game class that XNA Game Studio created for us. This class inherits from `Microsoft.Xna.Framework.Game`. This is our main game class. This class has some fields and methods that have been created for us.

Fields

Our game class has two fields, a GraphicsDeviceManager field and a SpriteBatch field. The GraphicsDeviceManager class will handle the configuration and management of our graphics card, so we don't have to. The SpriteBatch class we can use to draw 2D graphics.

Constructor

The constructor is called once at the start of the game. It creates a new GraphicsDeviceManager instance and sets the root directory for our content manager. This property will determine where the content is loaded from when calling Content.Load<>(""). We will use the content manager later on to load content. The constructor also sets the default framerate, being 30 frames per second for Windows Phone.

```
public MainGame()
{
    graphics = new GraphicsDeviceManager(this);
    Content.RootDirectory = "Content";
    // Frame rate is 30 fps by default for Windows Phone.
    TargetElapsedTime = TimeSpan.FromTicks(333333);
}
```

Initialize

We can use the Initialize method to initialize all non-graphics related content and query for services. By default, the Initialize method of the base class gets called. This makes sure all components are initialized as well. Make sure you create your objects before calling Initialize on the base class.

```
protected override void Initialize()
{
    // TODO: Add your initialization logic here

    base.Initialize();
}
```

LoadContent

We can use the LoadContent method to load our content. This will also be called once per game. In this method, we can use the content manager to load a variety of content—textures, models, and sounds for instance. By default, the spriteBatch field gets instantiated.

```
protected override void LoadContent()
{
    // Create a new SpriteBatch
    spriteBatch = new SpriteBatch(GraphicsDevice);
}
```

UnloadContent

We can use the `UnloadContent` method to unload any content. As most of the content we will use, uses the content pipeline, we won't have much use for this method. The `UnloadContent` method gets called once per game.

```
protected override void UnloadContent()
{
    // TODO: Unload any non ContentManager content here
}
```

Update

The `Update` method will run multiple times, and to be more specific, it will do its best to run 30 times per second (depending on the `TargetElapsedTime` property). In this method we will perform all calculations we need, such as collision detection, updating positions, playing sound, and gathering input. The method has one argument, an object of type `GameTime`. This object contains the total amount of time since the game started, as well as the time passed since the last update was called. We will use this object to make sure our game logic is frame rate independent. This means our object will move at the same speed, regardless the current frame rate—for example, if the `Update` method fails to be executed 30 times per second, we want our hero to move just as fast as if it were executing 30 times per second.

```
protected override void Update(GameTime gameTime)
{
    // Allows the game to exit
    if (GamePad.GetState(PlayerIndex.One).Buttons.Back ==
    ButtonState.Pressed)
        this.Exit();
    // TODO: Add your update logic here
    base.Update(gameTime);            .
}
```

Also note that in the `Update` method, we exit the game when the back button is pressed on the gamepad with index one. The interesting thing here is that the back button of the phone registers as the back button of the gamepad.

Draw

As the name suggests, we will use the `Draw` method to render our objects to the screen. By default, XNA will try to call this method 30 times per second on Windows Phone. Depending on how much you are drawing, this could be less. The method also has a `GameTime` object as argument, which provides a snapshot of the timing values. The first thing that happens in the method is that the graphics device gets cleared. Each time `Draw` is called, we render to a render target. A render target can be seen as a 2D image, or a whiteboard. Each time we want to draw a new frame, we need to clear the render target, or wipe the board. The `Clear` method takes a color as argument, by default cornflower blue. This means our background will be cornflower blue. After clearing our render target, we can draw all our graphics and call `Draw` on our base class. The default render target is the screen, but we don't have to worry about that just now.

```
protected override void Draw(GameTime gameTime)
{
    GraphicsDevice.Clear(Color.CornflowerBlue);

    // TODO: Add your drawing code here

    base.Draw(gameTime);
}
```

Summary

In this chapter, we've discussed the basics of Windows Phone game development and the XNA framework. We got started and installed all the tools we need to develop games on Windows Phone, registered our device so we could deploy to it and we created our first—be it limited—game!

Let's jump to the next chapter where we will learn how to draw sprites and display sprite animations on screen.

2D Graphics

2

In the previous chapter, we installed the necessary tools and set up our environment. We can now start by actually drawing some graphics.

In this chapter we will cover:

- The 2D coordinate system
- The content pipeline
- Loading and drawing sprites
- Translation, rotation, and scale of 2D objects
- Direction and movement

2D coordinate system

Before we start drawing, we need to have some knowledge about the 2D coordinate system. The 2D coordinate system uses two axes: x and y. The point of origin (being x = 0 and y = 0) is located at the top left corner. The x axis starts at 0 and increases to the right, and the y axis also starts at 0, but increases to the bottom. Note that the length of each axis is partly determined by the orientation.

Let's assume we have a device that supports an 800 X 480 resolution. In portrait, the x axis will be 480 pixels and the y axis 800. In landscape, x will be 800 pixels and y 480.

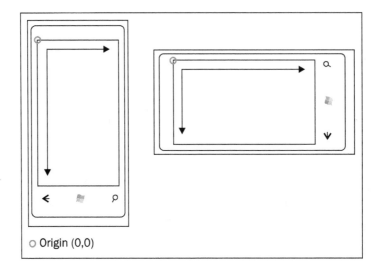

The orientation will change automatically depending on how you hold the device. By default, landscape left and landscape right are supported, as this does not affect our code. If we want to enable portrait as well, we can set the SupportedOrientations property of the graphics device manager.

```
graphics.SupportedOrientations = DisplayOrientation.Portrait |
                            DisplayOrientation.LandscapeLeft |
                            DisplayOrientation.LandscapeRight;
```

In this book, we will write all code for landscape. Note, that if you want to support portrait, you'll have to account for changing dimensions of the back buffer.

Adding content

Create a new project and call it Chapter2Demo. XNA Game Studio created a class called Game1. Rename it to MainGame so it has a proper name.

When we take a look at our solution, we can see two projects. A game project called Chapter2Demo that contains all our code, and a content project called Chapter2DemoContent. This content project will hold all our assets, and compile them to an intermediate file format (xnb). This is often done in game development to make sure our games start faster. The resulting files are uncompressed, and thus larger, but can be read directly into memory without extra processing.

Note that we can have more than one content project in a solution. We might add one per platform, but this is beyond the scope of this book.

Navigate to the content project using Windows Explorer, and place our textures in there.

 Downloading the example code

You can download the example code files for all Packt books you have purchased from your account at `http://www.packtpub.com`. If you purchased this book elsewhere, you can visit `http://www.packtpub.com/support` and register to have the files e-mailed directly to you.

The start files can be downloaded from the previously mentioned link. Then add the files to the content project by right-clicking on it in the Solution Explorer and choosing the **Add | Existing Item...**. Make sure to place the assets in a folder called `Game2D`.

When we click on the hero texture in the content project, we can see several properties. First of all, our texture has a name, **Hero**. We can use that name to load our texture in code. Note that this has no extension, because the files will be compiled to an intermediate format anyway.

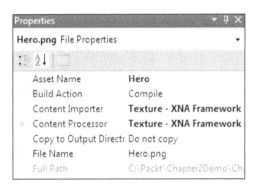

We can also specify a **Content Importer** and **Content Processor**. Our `.png` file gets recognized as texture so XNA Game studio automatically selects the **Texture** importer and processor for us. An importer will convert our assets into the "Content Document Object Model", a format that can be read by the processor. The processor will compile the asset into a managed code object, which can then be serialized into the intermediate `.xnb` file. That file will then be loaded at runtime. It is possible to write custom importers and processors, but this is beyond the scope of this book.

Drawing sprites

Everything is set up for us to begin. Let's start drawing some images. We'll draw a background, an enemy, and our hero.

Adding fields

At the top of our `MainGame`, we need to add a field for each of our objects. The type used here is `Texture2D`.

```
Texture2D _background, _enemy, _hero;
```

Loading textures

In the `LoadContent` method, we need to load our textures using the content manager.

```
// TODO: use this.Content to load your game content here
_background = Content.Load<Texture2D>("Game2D/Background");
_enemy = Content.Load<Texture2D>("Game2D/Enemy");
_hero = Content.Load<Texture2D>("Game2D/Hero");
```

The content manager has a generic method called `Load`. Generic meaning we can specify a type, in this case `Texture2D`. It has one argument, being the asset name. Note that you do not specify an extension, the asset name corresponds with the folder structure and then the name of the asset that you specified in the properties. This is because the content is compiled to `.xnb` format by our content project anyway, so the files we load with the content manager all have the same extension. Also note that we do not specify the root directory of our content, because we've set it in the game's constructor.

Drawing textures

Before we start drawing textures, we need to make sure our game runs in full screen. This is because the emulator has a bug and our sprites wouldn't show up correctly. You can enable full screen by adding the following code to the constructor:

```
graphics.IsFullScreen = true;
```

Now we can go to the `Draw` method. Rendering textures is always done in a specific way:

1. First we call the `SpriteBatch.Begin()` method. This will make sure all the correct states necessary for drawing 2D images are set properly.

2. Next we draw all our sprites using the `Draw` method of the sprite batch. This method has several overloads. The first is the texture to draw. The second an object of type `Vector2D` that will store the position of the object. And the last argument is a color that will tint your texture. Specify `Color.White` if you don't want to tint your texture.

3. Finally we call the `SpriteBatch.End()` method. This will sort all sprites we've rendered (according the the specified sort mode) and actually draw them.

If we apply the previous steps, they result in the following code:

```
// TODO: Add your drawing code here
spriteBatch.Begin();
spriteBatch.Draw(_background, new Vector2(0, 0), Color.White);
spriteBatch.Draw(_enemy, new Vector2(10, 10), Color.White);
spriteBatch.Draw(_hero, new Vector2(10, 348), Color.White);
spriteBatch.End();
```

Run the game by pressing *F5*. The result is shown in the following screenshot:

Refactoring our code

In the previous code, we've drawn three textures from our game class. We hardcoded the positions, something we shouldn't do. None of the textures were moving but if we want to add movement now, our game class would get cluttered, especially if we have many sprites. Therefore we will refactor our code and introduce some classes. We will create two classes: a `GameObject2D` class that is the base class for all 2D objects, and a `GameSprite` class, that will represent a sprite.

We will also create a `RenderContext` class. This class will hold our graphics device, sprite batch, and game time objects. We will use all these classes even more extensively when we begin building our own framework in *Chapter 6, Building a Basic Framework.*

Render context

Create a class called `RenderContext`. To create a new class, do the following:

1. Right-click on your solution.
2. Click on **Add | New Item**.
3. Select the **Code** template on the left.
4. Select **Class** and name it RenderContext.
5. Click on **OK**.

This class will contain three properties: `SpriteBatch`, `GraphicsDevice`, and `GameTime`. We will use an instance of this class to pass to the `Update` and `Draw` methods of all our objects. That way they can access the necessary information. Make sure the class has `public` as access specifier. The class is very simple:

```
public class RenderContext
{
    public SpriteBatch SpriteBatch { get; set; }
    public GraphicsDevice GraphicsDevice { get; set; }
    public GameTime GameTime { get; set; }
}
```

When you build this class, it will not recognize the terms `SpriteBatch`, `GraphicsDevice`, and `GameTime`. This is because they are stored in certain namespaces and we haven't told the compiler to look for them. Luckily, XNA Game Studio can find them for us automatically. If you hover over `SpriteBatch`, an icon like the one in the following screenshot will appear on the left-hand side. Click on it and choose the **using Microsoft.Xna.Framework.Graphics;** option. This will fix the `using` statement for you. Do it each time such a problem arises.

```
namespace Chapter2Demo
{
    public class RenderContext
    {
        public SpriteBatch SpriteBatch { get; set; }
        public      icsDevice GraphicsDevice { get; set; }
        public
                        using Microsoft.Xna.Framework.Graphics;
    }
}

                        Microsoft.Xna.Framework.Graphics.SpriteBatch

                        Generate class for 'SpriteBatch'
                        Generate new type...
```

The base class

The base class is called **GameObject2D**. The only thing it does is store the position, scale, and rotation of the object and a Boolean that determines if the object should be drawn. It also contains four methods: Initialize, LoadContent, Draw, and Update. These methods currently have an empty body, but objects that will inherit from this base class later on will add an implementation. We will also use this base class for our scene graph, so don't worry if it still looks a bit empty.

Properties

We need to create four automatic properties. The Position and the Scale parameters are of type Vector2. The rotation is a float and the property that determines if the object should be drawn is a bool.

```
public Vector2 Position { get; set; }

public Vector2 Scale { get; set; }

public float Rotation { get; set; }

public bool CanDraw { get; set; }
```

Constructor

In the constructor, we will set the Scale parameter to one (no scaling) and set the CanDraw parameter to true.

```
public GameObject2D()
{
    Scale = Vector2.One;
    CanDraw = true;
}
```

Methods

This class has four methods.

1. Initialize: We will create all our new objects in this method.

2. LoadContent: This method will be used for loading our content. It has one argument, being the content manager.

3. Update: This method shall be used for updating our positions and game logic. It also has one argument, the render context.

4. Draw: We will use this method to draw our 2D objects. It has one argument, the render context.

    ```
    public virtual void Initialize() { }

    public virtual void LoadContent(ContentManager contentManager) { }

    public virtual void Update(RenderContext renderContext) { }

    public virtual void Draw(RenderContext renderContext) { }
    ```

Building the GameSprite class

Now we can start building our sprite class. This class will **inherit** from GameObject2D In our previous example, we used a basic overload of the spritebatch Draw method. Since this class will be a general class that we can use a lot, we will make properties for each of the possible arguments.

Fields

Since we will be using this class to draw textures to screen, we will need to store the name of the texture we want to use and an object to load it in.

```
private readonly string _assetFile;
private Texture2D _texture;
```

Properties

A texture also has a width and a height. We may need this later on, so we will expose this as well.

```
public float Width { get { return _texture.Width; } }
public float Height { get { return _texture.Height; } }
```

Finally, we want to expose some arguments we can use when drawing the texture. We already know we can pass a color to the spritebatch Draw method that will tint the texture. We can also pass a depth, which will determine the order of drawing, a sprite effect that will enable us to flip our sprite, and a rectangle that will allow us to draw only part of a texture. This rectangle can be nullable (thus the question mark after the type). It has to be nullable because if we want to draw the entire texture, we have to pass null as argument to the Draw method.

```
public float Depth { get; set; }
public Color Color { get; set; }
public SpriteEffects Effect { get; set; }
public Rectangle? DrawRect { get; set; }
```

Constructor

In the constructor, we will store the name of the asset, set the color to white and add no sprite effects.

```
public GameSprite(string assetFile)
{
    _assetFile = assetFile;
    Color = Color.White;
    Effect = SpriteEffects.None;
}
```

Methods

Our sprite has two methods, LoadContent and Draw. We will use the LoadContent method to load our texture, just as we did in the first example.

```
public override void LoadContent(ContentManager contentManager)
{
    base.LoadContent(contentManager);
    _texture = contentManager.Load<Texture2D>(_assetFile);
}
```

In the `Draw` method, we will draw the object if and only if the `CanDraw` property is set to true.

```
public override void Draw(RenderContext renderContext)
{
    if (CanDraw)
    {
        renderContext.SpriteBatch.Draw(_texture, Position,
            DrawRect, Color, MathHelper.ToRadians(Rotation),
            Vector2.Zero, Scale, Effect, Depth);
        base.Draw(renderContext);
    }
}
```

Note that we are using the `SpriteBatch` property of the render context to draw the textures.

Updating MainGame

So now that we've created all the classes we need, it's time to implement them into our game.

Fields

Start by changing the type of the background, enemy, and hero to `GameSprite`. Also add a field type `RenderContext`.

```
GameSprite _background, _enemy, _hero;
RenderContext _renderContext;
```

Initialize

Here we will instantiate our render context. We will also instantiate our background, enemy, and hero. Finally we will set the position of the hero and the enemy, as these are now stored in the object itself.

```
protected override void Initialize()
{
    // TODO: Add your initialization logic here

    _renderContext = new RenderContext();

    _background = new GameSprite("Game2D/Background");
    _enemy = new GameSprite("Game2D/Enemy");
    _hero = new GameSprite("Game2D/Hero");
```

```
    _enemy.Position = new Vector2(10, 10);
    _hero.Position = new Vector2(10, 348);

    base.Initialize();
}
```

LoadContent

Here we set the SpriteBatch property and the GraphicsDevice property of our render context. We will also call LoadContent method on our hero, enemy, and background.

```
protected override void LoadContent()
{
    // Create a new SpriteBatch
    spriteBatch = new SpriteBatch(GraphicsDevice);

    // TODO: use this.Content to load your game content here
    _renderContext.SpriteBatch = spriteBatch;
    _renderContext.GraphicsDevice = graphics.GraphicsDevice;

    _background.LoadContent(Content);
    _enemy.LoadContent(Content);
    _hero.LoadContent(Content);
}
```

Update

In the Update method, we need to set the GameTime property of the render context. We will also call the Update method on our hero and the enemy. As the background will never move, we don't need to update it.

```
_renderContext.GameTime = gameTime;
_enemy.Update(_renderContext);
_hero.Update(_renderContext);
```

Draw

Finally in the `Draw` method, we will draw our background, enemy, and hero, passing the render context as argument.

```
spriteBatch.Begin();
_background.Draw(_renderContext);
_enemy.Draw(_renderContext);
_hero.Draw(_renderContext);
spriteBatch.End();
```

Result

When you run the game by pressing *F5*, you will see we have exactly the same result as before, but now we have a proper design. This way we can now easily add more functionality. Let's start by moving our hero.

Adding movement to the hero

We have a nice static scene now, but it doesn't make much of a game. Let's add some movement to the hero and make him walk over the screen. When he reaches an edge, he will turn back automatically.

The Hero2D class

So we want to add movement to the player. It is best to encapsulate all that new behavior in a class. Let's call class the `Hero2D`. This class will be responsible for loading the texture, updating the position, and drawing the texture. Make sure the class **inherits** from `GameObject2D` class. We could make it inherit from the `GameSprite` class, but we won't do that. Instead we will add a field of type `GameSprite`. This is called **composition**.

In the context of composition, Herb Sutter has said the following:

> *Prefer composition to inheritance*

The reasons why will become obvious when we implement the scene graph and when we make an animated sprite. For now, just go with it.

Fields

The class has three fields, a game sprite, a direction that determines if the player is going left or right, and the speed of movement. The direction is an integer and the speed is a constant integer. All fields can have the private access specifier.

```
private GameSprite _heroSprite;
private int _direction = 1; //Right = 1 | Left = -1
private const int Speed = 60; //px/sec
```

Initialize

In the `Initialize` method, we will make a new instance of the `GameSprite` class and assign it to the `_heroSprite` field. We will also set its position.

```
public override void Initialize()
{
    _heroSprite = new GameSprite("Game2D/Hero");
    _heroSprite.Position = new Vector2(10, 348);
}
```

LoadContent

In the `LoadContent` method, we will call the `LoadContent` method on the sprite.

```
public override void LoadContent(ContentManager contentManager)
{
    _heroSprite.LoadContent(contentManager);
}
```

Update

The update is responsible for moving the hero. We will only move the player about the x axis. This will appear as if the hero is walking on the ground plane. We need to implement the following steps.

1. As we will only calculate the distance the player has moved since the last update, we need to store the current position of the sprite in a temporary variable.

2. If the direction field is set to 1 (meaning we are moving to the right) and the position of the hero is bigger than the width of the screen minus the width of the hero (the hero is touching the right border of the screen), then we will negate the direction and set the sprite effect of our hero sprite to FlipHorizontally.

3. If the direction is minus one and the position of the sprite is less than zero, we will set the direction to one and stop applying a sprite effect.

4. Then we will add a delta to the x position of the hero. This delta will represent the movement and is calculated by multiplying speed, the elapsed game time, and the direction with each other. We multiply by the elapsed game time to make sure our hero moves at the same speed, regardless of the framerate.

5. Finally, set the position of the sprite.

```
public override void Update(RenderContext renderContext)
{
    var heroPos = _heroSprite.Position;

    if (_direction == 1 && heroPos.X >=
        renderContext.GraphicsDevice.Viewport.Width -
        (_heroSprite.Width * _heroSprite.Scale.X))
    {
        _direction = -1;
        _heroSprite.Effect = SpriteEffects.FlipHorizontally;
    }
    else if (_direction == -1 && heroPos.X < 0)
    {
        _direction = 1;
        _heroSprite.Effect = SpriteEffects.None;
    }

    heroPos.X += (float)(Speed
        * renderContext.GameTime.ElapsedGameTime.TotalSeconds
        * _direction);

    _heroSprite.Position = heroPos;
}
```

Draw

In the Draw method, we will simply draw the game sprite.

```
public override void Draw(RenderContext renderContext)
{
    _heroSprite.Draw(renderContext);
}
```

Updating the game class

In the game class, we need to use the new object. Therefore we must take care of the following steps:

1. Change the type of the hero field to Hero2D.

   ```
   Hero2D _hero;
   ```

2. In the Initialize method, create a new instance of the Hero2D class, initialize it and remove setting the position.

   ```
   _hero = new Hero2D();
   _hero.Initialize();

   //DELETE ME
   //_hero.Position = new Vector2(10, 380);
   ```

3. Press *F5* to see the result.

Result

The result should be a moving hero who turns around when he reaches the edge of the screen.

Adding animation to our hero

The following topics will guide us on adding animation to our hero.

Sprite sheets

As cool as a sliding hero might be, it would be nice to make him walk instead of slide. We can achieve this by using sprite sheets. A sprite sheet is an image that contains multiple versions of the character in a certain state (walking for example). We then render just a part of the sprite at a time. By switching the parts we render, we can make it appear as if the character is walking. In the following screenshot, you can see the sprite sheet that we will be using. It is 256 pixels wide and contains eight different frames. Each frame is 32 pixels wide by 39 pixels high. Note that it is also possible to have multiple rows in a single sprite sheet.

The GameAnimatedSprite class

The GameAnimatedSprite class is an extension of the GameSprite class. The extra functionality it will offer is drawing sprite animations, this means calculating which DrawRect to use (a parameter we use in our GameSprite class to draw the sprite), plus offering functionality to pause, play and loop animations. Make sure the class **inherits** from GameSprite.

Fields

A sprite sheet is a single texture that contains multiple columns and possibly multiple rows of a single texture. Therefore we need to store certain variables. The most obvious is the number of rows and columns. We also need a rectangle that represents which area to draw. Finally we will also store the total time the frame has been drawn. This is because we need to swap frames, and thus update the draw rectangle, at a given time.

```
private readonly int _rowCount;
private readonly int _columnCount;
private int _totalFrameTime;
private Rectangle _frameRect;
```

Properties

We also need some properties, values we need to be able to access from outside the class. We need to know how many frames there are in the sprite sheet, what size each frame is, what frame we are currently rendering, and also if we are currently playing an animation or if it is paused. These values can have a private setter because we don't want them to be modified outside this class. We also need the frame interval (how fast is the animation going) and a Boolean that determines if we should loop the animation.

```
public int NumFrames { get; private set; }
public Point FrameSize { get; private set; }
public int CurrentFrame { get; private set; }
public bool IsPlaying { get; private set; }
public bool IsPaused { get; private set; }

public int FrameInterval { get; set; }
public bool IsLooping { get; set; }
```

Constructors

We will have two constructors for this class, because the number of frames per row isn't really relevant when you have a sprite sheet that contains only one row. In that case the number of frames per row just equals the number of total frames. The shared arguments between the constructors are the asset file (which texture do we need to load) as string, the number of frames the sprite sheet contains, the interval at which the frames should be drawn, and finally, the size of a frame.

In the constructor without the number of frames per row, we just call the other constructor, passing the number of frames as the frames per row (as these two values are equal in case of a sprite sheet with only one row).

```
public GameAnimatedSprite(string assetFile, int numFrames, int
frameInterval, Point frameSize) :
    this(assetFile, numFrames, frameInterval, frameSize, numFrames) {
}
```

In the other constructor, we just store each value into our fields and properties. There are however some values we need to calculate.

- We need to set the width and height of the frame rectangle. This can be set to the frame size.

- The number of rows is 1, unless the number of frames per row is less than the total number of frames. If that is the case, the number of rows equals the number of frames divided by the number of frames per row. The column count is equal to the number of frames per row in that case.

```
public GameAnimatedSprite(string assetFile, int numFrames, int
frameInterval, Point frameSize, int framesPerRow) :
    base(assetFile)
{
    NumFrames = numFrames;
```

```
        FrameInterval = frameInterval;
        FrameSize = frameSize;

        _frameRect = new Rectangle(0, 0, frameSize.X, frameSize.Y);
        _rowCount = 1;
        _columnCount = numFrames;

        if (framesPerRow < numFrames)
        {
            _rowCount = numFrames / framesPerRow;
            _columnCount = framesPerRow;
        }

        DrawRect = _frameRect;
    }
```

Play, pause, and stop

When playing animations, we need to add some methods that will allow us to play, pause, and stop animations. These methods are very straight forward, as they just set properties to certain values. These properties will then be used in the update.

We will have two overloads of the method `PlayAnimation`. One that has one argument that specifies if we should loop the animation, and one without, where we assume we should not loop. The reason we are using overloads is that version 3 of C# (the one we can use to build Windows Phone games) does not support default parameters.

1. The method will check if the animation is paused. If so, set paused to false and return.

2. Otherwise, it will set the `IsPlaying` property to `true` and `IsLooping` property to the desired value.

```
public void PlayAnimation()
{
    PlayAnimation(false);
}

public void PlayAnimation(bool loop)
{
    if (IsPaused)
    {
        IsPaused = false;
        return;
```

```
        }

        IsPlaying = true;
        IsLooping = loop;
    }
```

The pause animation will set the `IsPaused` property to `true`. The stop animation will set the `IsPlaying` property to `false`, the CurrentFrame property to `0` and the `_totalFrameTime` field to `0` too.

```
public void StopAnimation()
{
    IsPlaying = false;
    CurrentFrame = 0;
    _totalFrameTime = 0;
}

public void PauzeAnimation()
{
    IsPaused = true;
}
```

Update

The `Update` method is where all the magic happens. If we are playing an animation and it is not paused, it will calculate a new rectangle. We will then use this rectangle to draw our texture (that code is already in `GameSprite`, where we use the `DrawRect` as argument when we draw the sprite).

1. Increment the total frame time with the time that passed since the last update was called (in milliseconds).

2. If the total frame time is greater or equal to our specified interval time, we can calculate the new frame. If not, we don't do any further calculations.

3. If we have a sprite sheet that has multiple rows, the location of the frame rectangle is set to a new point. The position of the rectangle will be the width and height of one frame multiplied by an offset. This will position our rectangle on the proper frame. To help you envision what's happening, let's assume the current frame is 10 and we have two rows and eight columns.

    The x position is the frame size multiplied by the remainder of the division of the current frame and the number of columns. In our example this would be the frame size multiplied by the remainder of 10/8, being 2. This will result in the third frame being drawn (remember, 0 based).

The y position will be the frame width multiplied by the division of the current frame with the number of frames per row (10/8) rounded down (meaning 0.99 results in 0). 10 divided by 8 will be rounded to 1, meaning we will shift one row down. We can use `Math.Floor` to round a double downwards.

4. If we don't have multiple rows, the code is a lot simpler. The location is simply a new point where the x value is the x size times the current frame, and the y value is 0. This will only shift the rectangle about the x axis.

5. Set the DrawRect property of the base class to the newly calculated frame rectangle.

6. Increment the current frame. Then if the current frame is greater-than-or-equal to the total number of frames, set the current frame to 0 and if we are looping, play again.

```
public override void Update(RenderContext renderContext)
{
    if (IsPlaying && !IsPaused)
    {
        _totalFrameTime += renderContext.GameTime.ElapsedGameTime.
Milliseconds;

        if (_totalFrameTime >= FrameInterval)
        {
            _totalFrameTime = 0;

            if (_rowCount > 1)
            {
                _frameRect.Location = new Point(
                    FrameSize.X *
                    (CurrentFrame % _columnCount),

                    FrameSize.Y * (int)Math.Floor(
                        CurrentFrame / _columnCount
                    )
                );
            }
            else _frameRect.Location = new Point(
                FrameSize.X * CurrentFrame, 0
            );

            DrawRect = _frameRect;

            ++CurrentFrame;
```

```
            if (CurrentFrame >= NumFrames)
            {
                CurrentFrame = 0;
                IsPlaying = IsLooping;
            }
        }
    }

    base.Update(renderContext);
}
```

Updating Hero2D

Finally, we need to update our Hero2D class so it uses the animated sprites.

Fields

Change the type of _heroSprite to GameAnimatedSprite and add a constant integer that represents the frame width.

```
private GameAnimatedSprite _heroSprite;
private const int FrameWidth = 32;
```

Initialize

Call the GameAnimatedSprite constructor and also enable animations.

```
_heroSprite = new GameAnimatedSprite("Game2D/Hero_Spritesheet"
    , 8, 80, new Point(FrameWidth,39));
_heroSprite.Position = new Vector2(10, 348);

_heroSprite.PlayAnimation(true);
```

Update

In the update, call the update method on the hero sprite.

```
_heroSprite.Update(renderContext);
```

Also, change the if where you check for the right border of the screen so it uses the frame width instead of the width of the texture.

```
if (_direction == 1 && heroPos.X >=
    renderContext.GraphicsDevice.Viewport.Width -
    (FrameWidth * _heroSprite.Scale.X))
```

Result

Instead of a sliding hero, your hero should be walking as a normal vampire would as shown in the following screenshot:

Summary

In this chapter, we've learned how to draw 2D images, move them around and use sprite animation. With this knowledge, we could go a lot further: we could make the enemy move and drop rocks (that fall because they are subject to "gravity" and "explode" on impact). We won't do that in this chapter as it uses the same knowledge as we've gained so far, but it is available in the resources that come with this book. If you want, you can take a look at it.

In the next chapter, we will leave the realm of 2D, and add an extra dimension. Let's start drawing 3D models!

3
3D Graphics

In the previous chapter, we explored the two-dimensional world. Now, we will add the third dimension.

In this chapter we will cover:

- The 3D coordinate system
- Local space and world space
- Matrices and the concept of world, view, and projection
- Loading and drawing 3D models
- Translation, rotation, and scale
- Skinned animations and skinned effect

3D coordinate system

Just like working in 2D, working in 3D means using a certain axis system. Unlike 2D, the coordinate system doesn't originate at the top left corner. But because we will be using a camera to view our scene, the origin doesn't matter that much.

If we hold the phone in landscape mode, the x axis is on the horizontal plane, the y axis on the vertical plane, and the z axis goes through the screen. This is known as a right-handed axis system.

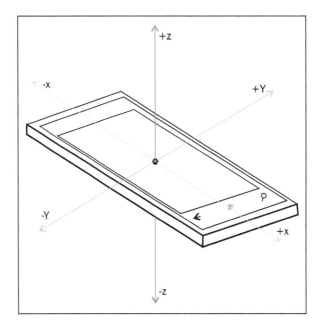

Using matrices

Matrices are used in 3D games a lot. The reason we use them is because they make our life easy. We could use regular trigonometry to map all our movement, but doing this for each axis would make it a hazardous task. Instead we can use matrices to wrap it all in one neat little package. We won't go into detail about how a matrix works, but we will explain how to use them. It is important however that we know what a matrix is: a matrix, or more specifically the four by four matrices we will be using, is a structure composed of 16 values that together define a transformation in 3D space. There are a couple of concepts we will come in contact with:

- **World**: A world matrix contains the position, the rotation, and the scale of an object.

- **View**: The view matrix contains the inverse of the camera's world matrix. This is because it will transform our vertices so they are seen from the camera.

- **Projection**: The projection matrix contains the lens settings of our camera.

If we want to position an object in a 3D world, and we want to see it from the camera's perspective, we need to pass the `WorldViewProjection` matrix to the effect. The `WorldViewProjection` matrix is the `World` matrix multiplied with the `View` and the `Projection` matrices; in that order!

Drawing models

There are several steps we need to take when drawing 3D models. Start by downloading the start files and open the `MainGame` class. Once this is done, we need to declare our `View` and `Projection` matrices. As these contain our camera settings, they will be the same for all 3D models. For each model, we'll need to add fields, load the model, and then draw it.

Adding fields

We'll create three fields: a field for the hero of type `Model`, and fields for the `View` and `Projection` matrices of type `Matrix`.

```
Model _hero;
Matrix _view, _projection;
```

Initialize

In the `Initialize` method, we will set the values for our `View` and `Projection` matrices.

1. We can create the `View` matrix by using the static `Matrix.CreateLookAt` method. It has three arguments. The first is the position of the camera, the second what it's looking at, and the third the up vector. We will place the camera 20 units along the positive z axis, pointed back at the origin.

2. For the `Projection` matrix we will use an orthographic projection. This means that, unlike perspective, the objects remain the same size regardless of the distance from the camera. We can create an orthographic projection matrix by using the static `Matrix.CreateOrthographic` method. The method has four arguments: the width of the projection, the height of the projection, the near plane, and the far plane, as illustrated in the following figure. Everything in front of the near plane and behind the far plane will not be visible.

```
_view = Matrix.CreateLookAt(new Vector3(0, 0, 20),
          new Vector3(0, 0, 0), Vector3.Up);
_projection = Matrix.CreateOrthographic(800, 480, 0.1f, 300);
```

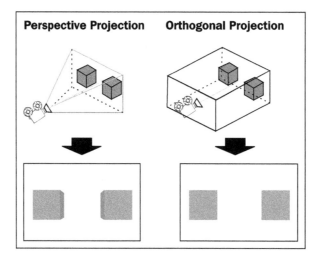

Note that games usually have a perspective projection, but because we are mixing 2D and 3D, orthogonal is the better choice.

Loading models

Loading models is very similar to as loading textures. Instead of loading an object of type `Texture2D` we will load an object of type `Model`.

```
_hero = Content.Load<Model>("Game3D/Vampire");
```

Let us take a minute to talk about what a `Model` is in XNA. A model is a representation of a logical entity, such as a person or a car. A model contains a container of `ModelMesh` objects. A `ModelMesh` represents a single physical object that can be moved or drawn independently from the others (for example, the arm of a person). A `ModelMesh` contains several `ModelMeshParts`, which are lists of triangles that use the same material (for example, the same texture). The `Model` class also contains a list of `Bones`, those describe the positioning of the `ModelMesh` items. A lot of explanation, so let us jump into drawing the model to get a better understanding of this.

Drawing models

Drawing models is a bit more work than drawing textures. We need to follow several steps.

1. We need to copy the bone transforms to a temporary matrix variable. A model can, as explained previously, contains several bones, which have a transform relative to the parent bone; this is called a bone transform. A bone transform can be visualized as a World matrix for each bone.

2. A model can contain several meshes, so we need to loop over all the meshes inside the model.

3. Every mesh can have multiple effects, so we need to loop over them as well. An effect is a class that is used to set properties on a shader. A shader is a program, or a piece of code, that runs on the graphics card that defines how an object should look, while transforming the 3D model into an image.

4. For each effect we need to set the `World`, `View` and `Projection` matrices, so the shader can transform our vertices on the graphics card. We will also enable the default lighting, so our model is actually lit.

5. Finally, we can draw the mesh.

```
var transforms = new Matrix[_hero.Bones.Count];
_hero.CopyAbsoluteBoneTransformsTo(transforms);

foreach (ModelMesh mesh in _hero.Meshes)
{
    foreach (BasicEffect effect in mesh.Effects)
    {
        effect.EnableDefaultLighting();

        effect.View = _view;
        effect.Projection = _projection;
        effect.World = transforms[mesh.ParentBone.Index];
    }

    mesh.Draw();
}
```

Result

The result should be the hero, in T-pose, located in the middle of the screen, as illustrated in the following screenshot:

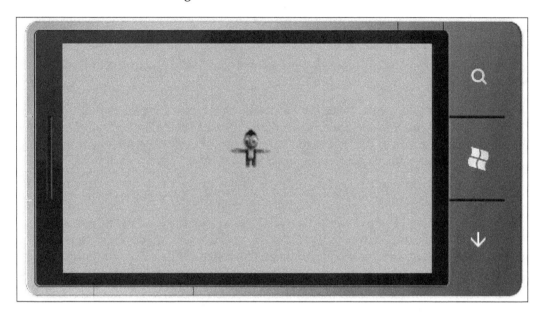

Mixing 2D and 3D

One thing we need to know when mixing 2D and 3D is that the order of drawing is important. If we draw our 2D graphics last, they will be in front of our models. This can be necessary for the HUD (heads up display) for instance. A background however needs to be behind the model, so we need to draw it first.

Also, calling the End method on a SpriteBatch object doesn't reset the states. We need to do this manually, and if we don't, our model won't appear correctly. We need to set the blend state, the depth stencil state, and the sampler states before drawing the model. The blend state controls how colors are blended, or mixed, together. The depth stencil state controls how depth impacts rendering (if we don't set this, our model will have no depth). And finally, the sampler state defines how textures are sampled, including the method of filtering and level of detail.

```
graphics.GraphicsDevice.BlendState = BlendState.Opaque;
graphics.GraphicsDevice.DepthStencilState =
  DepthStencilState.Default;
graphics.GraphicsDevice.SamplerStates[0] =
  SamplerState.LinearWrap;
```

As an exercise, try drawing the background behind our hero. The result should look like the following screenshot:

Refactoring our code

Just like with 2D, we need to refactor our code so it remains clean. We've drawn one model now, but if we were to draw many models and add movement to them, our code would get cluttered. So we will add some classes in the same manner as we did with 2D.

The base class

The base class for all our 3D objects is called GameObject3D. This class will contain the position, rotation, and scale of the object, along with the necessary methods to initialize, update, and draw models. This class is abstract, because we don't need to be able to instantiate it.

Properties

This class will have four properties, of which three are public. The position, rotation, and scale are public, while the `World` matrix is protected (the `World` matrix is the compiled version of the position, rotation, and scale, as explained in the previous section). The rotation is of type `Quaternion`, a structure that has four components, and very suited for holding rotations, because unlike matrices it avoids gimbal lock (gimbal lock is the loss of a degree of freedom that occurs when two axes become parallel).

```
public Vector3 Position { get; set; }
public Quaternion Rotation { get; set; }
public Vector3 Scale { get; set; }
protected Matrix WorldMatrix;
```

Constructor

In the constructor, we just need to initialize the scale to one (the default value for scale).

```
Scale = Vector3.One;
```

Methods

Just like the `GameObject2D` class, `GameObject3D` class also has methods for initializing, loading content, updating, and drawing. All methods are empty except for the `Update` method. In that method, we need to calculate the `World` matrix of the object. This can be done by multiplying the rotation matrix, with the scale matrix and the position matrix (in that order). Again, we transform our rotation, scale, and position to matrices because they can easily be multiplied together.

```
public virtual void Initialize() { }

public virtual void LoadContent(ContentManager contentManager) { }

public virtual void Update(RenderContext renderContext)
{
    WorldMatrix = Matrix.CreateFromQuaternion(Rotation) *
                  Matrix.CreateScale(Scale) *
                  Matrix.CreateTranslation(Position);
}

public virtual void Draw(RenderContext renderContext) { }
```

The camera

Let's also make a class for the camera. The camera will inherit from `GameObject3D` and will have two fields of type `Matrix`, for the `View` and the `Projection` matrices.

```
public class Camera : GameObject3D
{
    public Matrix View { get; protected set; }
    public Matrix Projection { get; protected set; }
}
```

In the **constructor**, we will set the projection to the same orthographic projection we had in the previous demo.

```
Projection = Matrix.CreateOrthographic(800, 480, 0.1f, 300);
```

Finally, in the `Update` method, we need to calculate the view matrix. We will use the position from the base class as position, and use the rotation to calculate the `lookat` value. The `lookat` is the target the camera will be looking at. If we transform the forward vector (`Vector3.Forward`) with the rotation of our camera, we will look in the direction we turned. One thing we need to do is to normalize the result, so the vector has a length of one.

```
var lookAt = Vector3.Transform(Vector3.Forward, Rotation);
lookAt.Normalize();

View = Matrix.CreateLookAt(Position, (Position + lookAt), Vector3.Up);
```

Updating RenderContext

Since our camera holds the view and projection matrix, which every 3D object needs, we will need a way of transferring it. The solution is adding an extra property to the render context; that property being our camera. This will then get passed to the `update` and `draw` methods of all our 3D objects.

```
public Camera Camera { get; set; }
```

The GameModel

Now we can start by building our model class. This class will **inherit** from `GameObject3D`, and is very similar to the `GameSprite` class; except it will handle drawing models.

Fields

This class will have two fields, one for the path to the asset and one of type `Model` that will hold the model.

```
private readonly string _assetFile;
private Model _model;
```

Constructor

In the constructor, we will only store the path to the model.

```
public GameModel(string assetFile)
{
    _assetFile = assetFile;
}
```

Methods

In this class we will override two methods, the `LoadContent` and `Draw` method. In the `LoadContent` method, we will load our model. In the `Draw` method, we will draw it. The only difference between this code and the previous is that we now use the `View` and `Projection` matrices of our camera, and we multiply the bone transform with the `World` matrix of the object (to move it around in the world).

```
public override void LoadContent(ContentManager contentManager)
{
    _model = contentManager.Load<Model>(_assetFile);

    base.LoadContent(contentManager);
}

public override void Draw(RenderContext renderContext)
{
    var transforms = new Matrix[_model.Bones.Count];
    _model.CopyAbsoluteBoneTransformsTo(transforms);

    foreach (ModelMesh mesh in _model.Meshes)
    {
        foreach (BasicEffect effect in mesh.Effects)
        {
            effect.EnableDefaultLighting();

            effect.View = renderContext.Camera.View;
            effect.Projection =
            renderContext.Camera.Projection;
```

```
            effect.World = transforms[mesh.ParentBone.Index] *
        WorldMatrix;
    }

    mesh.Draw();
}

base.Draw(renderContext);
}
```

Updating MainGame

So we've created all the classes we need; now it's time to implement them in our game.

Fields

We need to change the type of _hero to GameModel and create a field for our camera.

```
GameModel _hero;
Camera _camera;
```

Initialize

In the Initialize method, we need to instantiate our camera, and hero. We also want to move the camera 20 units along the z axis, and store it in the render context. Finally, we also need to translate our hero so it is positioned on the ground plane of the background.

```
_camera = new Camera();
_camera.Position = new Vector3(0, 0, 20);

_renderContext.Camera = _camera;

_hero = new GameModel("Game3D/Vampire");
_hero.Position = new Vector3(0, -147, -100);
```

LoadContent, Update, and Draw

We need to call LoadContent, Update, and Draw on our hero in respectively the LoadContent, Update, and Draw method. Also, we must not forget to update our camera.

Result

When we run the game by pressing *F5*, we will see we have pretty much the same result as before, but now we have a proper design. This way we can now easily add more functionality. Let's start by moving our hero.

Adding movement to the hero

Just like in the previous chapter, we will now add movement to our hero. He'll walk over the ground plane and turn around when he reaches the edge of the screen.

The Hero3D class

We'll start by creating a Hero3D class that will encapsulate all the behavior for movement. This class will **inherit** from GameObject3D class, and just like Hero2D, we will use composition.

Fields

The class has three fields, the model, the direction in which the player will move, and the walk speed.

```
private GameModel _heroModel;
private int _direction = 1; //1 = Right / -1 = Left
private const int Speed = 75;
```

Initialize

In the `Initialize` method we will create a new `GameModel` instance and set its position.

```
_heroModel = new GameModel("Game3D/Vampire");
_heroModel.Position = new Vector3(0, -147, -100);
```

LoadContent and Draw

In the `LoadContent` and `Draw` methods we just call `LoadContent` and `Draw` methods on `_heroModel`.

Update

The update is where all the magic happens. In this method, we will calculate the new position and rotation of our hero. We need to implement several steps:

1. As we will only calculate the distance the player has moved since the last update, we need to store the current position of the model in a temporary variable.

2. In 2D, we can just check the position of the player with the width of our viewport. In 3D it is not that simple; because our camera and model can be anywhere in 3D space, we need to transform the position of the hero so it is in screen space instead of world space, as illustrated in the following image. We can do this by using the `Project` method of the `Viewport` class, passing the position along with the view and projection matrices.

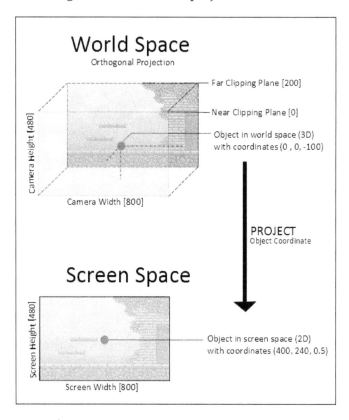

3. If the direction field is set to 1 (meaning we are moving to the right) and the x value of the projected vector is bigger than the width of the screen (the hero is touching the right border of the screen), then we will negate the direction. Note that we currently disregard the width of the player, so half of the player will be exiting the screen before he turns.

4. If the direction is minus one and the x value of the projected vector is less than zero, we will set the direction to one.

5. Next we need to update the position. We do this by multiplying `Vector3. Right` (so we only move on the horizontal plane) with the speed, the elapsed time and the direction. `Vector3.Right` is a vector with 1 as x value and 0 as y and z-value.

6. Depending on which way we are moving, we need to rotate the player 90 degrees or minus 90 degrees about the y axis. Since our direction is either `1` or `-1`, we can use this. The only problem in the rotation of our hero is a quaternion, so we need to use the static `CreateFromYawPitchRoll` method to calculate the quaternion. Since we are rotating about the y axis, we need to set the yaw. And we must not forget to use radians! Yaw, pitch, and roll come from flight dynamics and are angles of rotation about the center of mass.

7. Finally, we still need to call the `Update` method on the `hero` model so the `World` matrix is calculated properly. Otherwise our hero would not move.

```
public override void Update(RenderContext renderContext)
{
    var heroPos = _heroModel.Position;
    var projVec =
            renderContext.GraphicsDevice.Viewport.Project(
            heroPos, renderContext.Camera.Projection,
            renderContext.Camera.View, Matrix.Identity);

    if (_direction == 1 && projVec.X >=
        renderContext.GraphicsDevice.Viewport.Width)
    {
        _direction = -1;
    }
    else if (_direction == -1 && projVec.X <= 0)
    {
        _direction = 1;
    }

    heroPos += Vector3.Right * (float)(Speed *
        renderContext.GameTime.ElapsedGameTime.TotalSeconds *
        _direction);
    _heroModel.Position = heroPos;
    _heroModel.Rotation = Quaternion.CreateFromYawPitchRoll(
        MathHelper.ToRadians(90 * _direction), 0, 0);

    _heroModel.Update(renderContext);
}
```

Updating the Game class

We also need to update the `Game` class so we use our `Hero3D` instead of a regular game model. Don't forget to call `Initialize`, `LoadContent`, `Update`, and `Draw` methods.

Result

The result should be a moving (sliding) hero who turns around when he reaches the edge of the screen.

Adding animation to our hero

We didn't like it in *Chapter 2, 2D Graphics*, and we still don't like the sliding hero. Time to add animation!

We have a small problem however: XNA has an effect that supports skinned animations, but it's not included in the base XNA installation. Luckily these have been made available through the Dev Center. Skinned animation is a technique that has a visual representation of a model, and a set of bones used to animate the model. As this fits with the implementation of the Model class, we will use this technique. When taking a look at the start project for animation that comes with this chapter, we can see that the solution has two extra projects: a SkinnedModelPipeline project and a SkinnedModelData project. The first contains a processor that will compile our model taking the animations into account. It has also been updated with Shawn Hargreaves' method for merging multiple .fbx animations into one file. Note that hero model uses this SkinnedModelProcessor, otherwise animation would not work. The SkinnedModelData project holds the classes we will use to play the animations.

Asset Name	**Enemy**
Build Action	Compile
Content Importer	**X File - XNA Framework**
▷ Content Processor	**SkinnedModelProcessor**
Copy to Output Directory	Copy if newer
File Name	Enemy.x
Full Path	C:\Packt\Design your first mobile

The GameAnimatedModel class

The GameAnimatedModel class is a lot like the GameModel class. It inherits from GameObject3D class. This class has already been added to the start files and Hero3D has been updated to use it instead of the GameModel class.

Currently, this class has two fields: a model and the asset file. LoadContent, Draw, and Update are also in there. The following code will just handle the changes specific for animation.

Fields

We need to add three fields: one for the animation player which will be responsible for playing the animations, one for the skinning data that holds the animation data, and one to set the speed of the animation.

```
private AnimationPlayer _animationPlayer;
private SkinningData _skinningData;
private float _speedScale = 1f;
```

LoadContent

After loading the model, we need to retrieve the skinning data from it. We can then use the skinning data to create a new instance of the animation player, and set the default animation speed to 1.

```
_skinningData = _model.Tag as SkinningData;

Debug.Assert(_skinningData != null,
    "Model (" + _assetFile + ") contains no Skinning Data!");

_animationPlayer = new AnimationPlayer(_skinningData);
_animationPlayer.SetAnimationSpeed(_speedScale);
```

Update

If we are playing an animation, we need to update it every frame, passing the elapsed game time and the world matrix.

```
if (_animationPlayer.CurrentClip != null)
    _animationPlayer.Update(
    renderContext.GameTime.ElapsedGameTime, true,
    WorldMatrix);
```

Controlling animations

The animation player enables us to control the animation. We will want to expose some of this behavior, so whoever is using the GameAnimatedModel class can control the animation as well. We'll need to implement three methods.

- We'll need to implement a method that enables us to play animations. The animation player exposes this functionality via the StartClip method that has one argument of type Clip. We can retrieve this clip from the skinning data we stored when we loaded the content.

- The animation player offers support for setting the speed of the animation, we'll need to expose this as well.

- An animated model has several bones, that all have their own transform. Sometimes, we might want to attach an object to a specific bone; for example a sword to a player's hand, or a rock in an enemy's hand. Therefore we must create a method that returns the transform for a specific bone. The animation player has a method called `GetBoneTransform`, which does just that.

```
public void PlayAnimation(string clipName)
{
    Debug.Assert(
      _skinningData.AnimationClips.ContainsKey(clipName),
      string.Format("No animation {0} found", clipName));

      var clip = _skinningData.AnimationClips[clipName];
      _animationPlayer.StartClip(clip);
}


public void SetAnimationSpeed(float speedScale)
{
    if (_animationPlayer != null)
        _animationPlayer.SetAnimationSpeed(speedScale);

    _speedScale = speedScale;
}


public Matrix GetBoneTransform(string boneName)
{
    if (_animationPlayer != null)
        return _animationPlayer.GetBoneTransform(boneName);

    return Matrix.Identity;
}
```

Draw

Drawing animated models is very similar to drawing regular models. We only need to do some extra steps, like sending the transforms of each bone to the effect. We will also not be using the basic effect to draw the model, but a skinned effect. Overall, we need to implement the following steps:

1. First of all, we need to store the transforms of each bone. We can do this by using the `GetSkinTransforms` method of the animation player.

2. We need to loop over each mesh inside our model, and over each skinned effect inside each mesh. If we are playing animations, we need to copy the bone transforms to our effect, otherwise we need to set the world matrix as we normally do. Finally, we need to enable default lighting and set the view matrix, projection matrix, specular color, and specular power. Specular is the light a model reflects when lit. The higher the specular power, the smaller the highlight.

3. Finally we need to draw the mesh.

```
public override void Draw(RenderContext renderContext)
{
    Matrix[] bones = null;
    if (_animationPlayer.CurrentClip != null)
        bones = _animationPlayer.GetSkinTransforms();

    foreach (ModelMesh mesh in _model.Meshes)
    {
        foreach (SkinnedEffect effect in mesh.Effects)
        {
            if (_animationPlayer.CurrentClip != null)
                effect.SetBoneTransforms(bones);
            else
                effect.World = WorldMatrix;

            effect.EnableDefaultLighting();

            effect.View = renderContext.Camera.View;
            effect.Projection =
          renderContext.Camera.Projection;

            effect.SpecularColor = new Vector3(0.25f);
            effect.SpecularPower = 16;
        }

        mesh.Draw();
    }

    base.Draw(renderContext);
}
```

Updating Hero3D

To update the `Hero3D` class so that making use of the animated model is very straightforward. We need to take the following steps:

1. Change the type of `_heroModel` from `GameModel` to `GameAnimatedModel`. We need to do this for the field and in the `Initialize` method.

2. In the `LoadContent` class, after calling `LoadContent` method on our hero model, we can start the animation.

    ```
    _heroModel.PlayAnimation("Run");
    ```

Result

Instead of a sliding hero, our hero should be walking as a normal 3D vampire would as shown in the following screenshot:

Exercise: adding enemies

As an exercise, we can update this demo so we include the enemy, and just as the previous demo make him drop rocks at the player.

 For attaching the rock to the hero, use the `GetBoneTransform` method of our `GameAnimatedModel` class. As usual, the solution can be found with the companion files.

Summary

In this chapter, we've covered drawing 3D models, both static and animated. In order to be able to do this, we covered the 3D coordinate system and brushed up our matrices. Mixing 2D and 3D shouldn't be an issue anymore.

However up until now, we haven't had interaction with our player, which is quite important for games. That's about to change in the next chapter!

4
Input

In the previous chapters, we've covered graphics, drawing 2D sprites, and 3D models. By doing this we can make pretty visualizations and simulations, but games need interaction with the user. Therefore we need to handle input from the user.

In this chapter, we will cover the various input possibilities:

- Keyboard
- Accelerometer
- Touch
- Gestures

Using keyboard

Sometimes it might be handy to have the player enter some text on the keyboard, for instance for entering the player name or the high score. Most Windows Phone 7 devices don't have a physical keyboard, so we will have to make an on-screen keyboard pop up. Luckily, this is very simple, as the static `Guide` class exposes this functionality. The `Guide` class has a static method `BeginShowKeyboardInput`. This method can be used to pop up the on screen keyboard. The fact that the method name starts with begin shows that it is an asynchronous method. This means the game keeps running the game loop cycles while the keyboard is visible. The method has six arguments:

- The player index: This is because Windows Phone only supports one player, this will always be one.
- The title of the dialog box.
- The description of the dialog box.
- The default text to show in the input text field.

- The callback method that should be called when the operation is finished, by pressing the **OK** or **Cancel** button.

- A state object: This is a user created object that identifies this request. Common practice is to pass `null`.

It's always a good idea to check if the keyboard isn't visible before calling the `BeginShowKeyboardInput` method.

```
if (!Guide.IsVisible)
{
    Guide.BeginShowKeyboardInput(PlayerIndex.One,
        "What is the hero's name?",
        "Choose a name for the hero, Nosferatu or Dracula?",
        "Nosferatu?", EndShowKeyboardCallback, null);
}
```

The callback is a method that will be called when the operation has finished. It has void as return type and an `IAsyncResult` object as argument. In the callback, we can use the `EndShowKeyboardInput` method to get the text that was entered.

```
private void EndShowKeyboardCallback(IAsyncResult result)
{
    string _heroName =
        Guide.EndShowKeyboardInput(result) ?? "Nosferatu";
}
```

The `??` operator in the previous code sets the default value in case the return value of the `EndShowKeyboardInput` method is `null`. This is because when we press **OK**, the contents of the input line are returned; otherwise `null` is returned.

In the sample accompanying this chapter, we pop up the keyboard when you tap the screen, and print the hero name you entered.

Using the accelerometer

Amongst the Windows Phone 7 hardware sensors is the accelerometer. This sensor can be used to detect tilt in three dimensions. Some games, like maze games, are very suited for using the accelerometer as an input device for movement. XNA Game Studio doesn't support the accelerometer by default; instead we have to add a reference to `Microsoft.Devices.Sensors` manually. We can do this by right-clicking our solution and choosing **Add Reference**. After we have added the reference, we can make a new instance of the `Accelerometer` class (if the device supports the accelerometer). Note that you can have no more than ten instances of the `Accelerometer` class. This class has support for starting and stopping the accelerometer, along with an event handler called `CurrentValueChanged`. This event handler is called each time the accelerometer detects a new value.

The code is fairly straight forward:

```
if (Accelerometer.IsSupported)
{
    // Max 10 simultanious instances
    var _accelerometer = new Accelerometer();

    // Add the event handler to the sensor.
    _accelerometer.CurrentValueChanged +=
        new EventHandler<
        SensorReadingEventArgs<AccelerometerReading>
        > (AccelerometerReadingChanged);
    // Start.
    _accelerometer.Start();
}
```

In the event handler, the current acceleration vector is made available through the event arguments.

```
void AccelerometerReadingChanged(object sender, SensorReadingEventArgs
<AccelerometerReading> e)
{
    Vector3 reading = e.SensorReading.Acceleration;
}
```

In the previous example, reading is a Vector3 that contains the current acceleration. The accelerometer has a custom axis system. When the phone is in landscape mode, the x axis is vertical, the y axis is horizontal and the z axis runs in the depth. Note the positive and negative direction illustrated in the following screenshot. Also, the axis system of the accelerometer doesn't change whether you hold the phone in landscape or portrait mode; the term landscape is used so that you have a reference to the vertical and horizontal directions in the explanation.

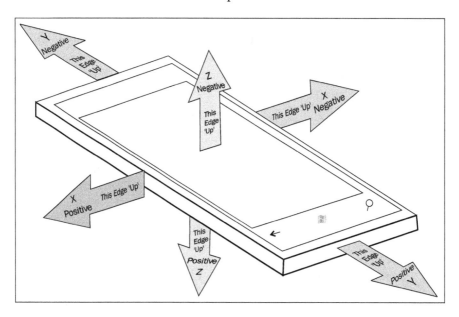

Finally, it's always good practice to stop the accelerometer when you are not using it, for example when the game is paused.

In the accompanying example, we've updated our 2D game so the accelerometer influences the movement of our hero.

Using touch

As Windows Phone devices have a touch screen, XNA Game Studio also offers support for (multi-)touch. This is fairly straight forward and all managed by the static TouchPanel class. Good practice when starting your game is to check the capabilities of the device, like the maximum touch count. That way we can be sure that the device meets our expectations. We can do this by using the static GetCapabilities method.

```
TouchPanelCapabilities tc = TouchPanel.GetCapabilities();
if (tc.IsConnected)
```

```
{
    return tc.MaximumTouchCount;
}
```

Looping over all touch locations is also very straight forward. The static class `TouchPanel` has a `GetState` method that returns a `TouchCollection`. This collection contains `TouchLocations`. We can use those to get the positions we need. Note that we should only call the `GetState` method once per frame; otherwise calling the `GetState` method twice will return refreshed data, resulting in missed events.

```
TouchCollection touchCollection = TouchPanel.GetState();
foreach (TouchLocation tl in touchCollection)
{
    Vector2 tempPos = tl.Position;
}
```

In the demo accompanying this chapter we change the y position of the hero according to the touch position.

Gestures

Windows Phone has support for touch-based gestures, and this support is also exposed through XNA Game studio. This means we can take advantage of them in our games without having to implement the gestures ourselves. In the following section, you can find a list of all supported gestures. Note that the only multi-touch gesture is pinch.

- **Tap**: a tap on the screen (touch and release)
- **DoubleTap**: two taps in short succession
- **Hold**: a finger touches the screen for a brief period
- **FreeDrag**: a finger touches the screen and moves in any direction
- **HorizontalDrag**: a finger touches the screen and moves about the horizontal axis
- **VerticalDrag**: a finger touches the screen and moves about the vertical axis
- **DragComplete**: end of FreeDrag, HorizontalDrag, or VerticalDrag
- **Flick**: drag finger across screen and lift without stopping the drag
- **Pinch**: two fingers move around the screen
- **PinchComplete**: end of Pinch

Enabling gestures

The static `TouchPanel` class has a property called `EnabledGestures`. With this property, you can enable any of the previous gestures. In the following example, we enable `DoubleTap` and `VerticalDrag`.

```
TouchPanel.EnabledGestures = GestureType.DoubleTap
    | GestureType.VerticalDrag;
```

Note that it's good practice to only enable the gestures that we want to respond to at a certain time.

Reading gestures

In the update, we can easily check if the user made a gesture on the touch panel. The `TouchPanel` class has a static property called `IsGestureAvailable`. If it is set to `true`, we can use the static `ReadGesture` method to get the gesture. Based on the gesture type, we can apply certain actions. In the following code, we capture the vertical drag and the double tap. Note that the vertical drag has a position and a delta, while the double tap will only have a position (the other properties will not be used).

```
while (TouchPanel.IsGestureAvailable)
{
    GestureSample gs = TouchPanel.ReadGesture();
    switch (gs.GestureType)
    {
        case GestureType.VerticalDrag:
            Vector2 dragPos = gs.Position;
            Vector2 dragDelta = gs.Delta;
            break;

        case GestureType.DoubleTap:
            Vector2 tapPos = gs.Position;
            break;
    }
}
```

In the gesture example accompanying this book, we switch the direction of our hero on double tap, and move our hero up and down on vertical drag.

Summary

In this chapter, we've covered the possible ways of gathering input from the user. This enables us to add interaction to our games and actually control our hero.

Next, we will explore the realm of audio. Audio and sounds will help set the mood for our game and make certain actions more clear to the player. Let's go!

5
Sound

In the previous chapters, we've covered all the basics we need to write games. One important part is missing though: sound. Sound will help set the mood for our game, and is thus a very important aspect.

In this chapter we will cover:

- Loading sounds
- Playing sounds
- Looping sounds
- Adjusting pitch and volume
- Playing 3D sounds
- Playing songs from the media library

Before we start

There are several ways to play sounds or music in XNA. The `SoundEffect` and `SoundEffectInstance` classes enable us to do just that. XACT, Microsoft cross platform audio creation tool, is not supported on Windows Phone. However, there is still a lot we can do with the classes that are provided from the XNA framework, such as playing sounds, playing 3D sounds adjusting volume, pitch, and so on. There is no real limit on how many sounds you can load, except memory of the device of course. There is however a limit on how many sounds you can play simultaneously, that is 64. If we try to play more than 64 sounds at once, we will get an exception.

Let's start by playing some sounds! The sounds we will use in the demos come from `flashkit.com` and are freeware.

Playing sound

Playing non-positional sounds, being regular sounds, is fairly straight forward. XNA contains a class called `SoundEffect`. This class can load sounds and play them. Let's jump into a sample.

SoundEffect

The code files contain all the audio samples we need. Add them to your content project. The importer and processor will be automatically detected by XNA Game Studio, depending on the file type. WAV files will use the `SoundEffect` processor by default, while MP3 files will use the `Song` processor by default.

Then in the `MainGame`, we need to create a field that will hold the sound. This field will be of type `SoundEffect`. Also add a counter of type `int`. We will play the sound if the counter reaches 100.

```
SoundEffect jumpSound;
int counter = 0;
```

In the `LoadContent` method, we have to load the sound. This is done in the same fashion as loading other content.

```
jumpSound = Content.Load<SoundEffect>("Jump");
```

Finally, in the update, we'll increment the counter. If the counter reaches `100`, we will play the sound using `SoundEffect.Play` method.

```
counter++;
if (counter >= 100)
{
    counter = 0;
    jumpSound.Play();
}
```

When you press *F5*, you should hear the sound periodically when the emulator has loaded our game.

Setting volume, pitch, and pan

The `Play` method of the `SoundEffect` class has another overload where we can specify the volume, pitch, and pan.

The volume is a float value from 0.0 to 1.0. Complete silence is 0.0 and full volume (relative to the `SoundEffect.MasterVolume` property) is 1.0. So a value of 1.0 will make the sound play at the current volume level of the device.

The pitch, or the frequency of the sound, is a value from -1.0 to 1.0. The normal pitch is 0.0, -1.0 is an octave down, and 1.0 is an octave up.

The pan is a value ranging from -1.0 to 1.0. Again, 0.0 is the normal situation, being centered. -1.0 plays fully through the left speaker and 1.0 fully through the right.

If you change the play code to the following code, the sound will play at half the volume, one octave higher end fully through the left speaker. Note that panning may not work on an actual device unless headphones are used. A phone with one centralized speaker will not pan.

```
jumpSound.Play(0.5f,1.0f,-1.0f);
```

The problem with `SoundEffect` is that it is a play and forget about it sound. After you call play, you can't modify the sound. The `SoundEffectInstance` fixes this issue.

SoundEffectInstance

If you want more control over your sounds, you can use the `SoundEffectInstance` class. This class has properties for setting volume, pitch, pan, and looping. It also has functionality for playing, stopping, pausing, and resuming the sound. You can play multiple `SoundEffectInstance` objects from one `SoundEffect` object. In the following code, we will recreate the demo from the previous section, but we will use a `SoundEffectInstance` class.

Fields

We will create two fields, one for the sound effect and one for the instance.

```
SoundEffect jumpSound;
SoundEffectInstance jumpInstance;
```

LoadContent

In the `LoadContent` method, we will perform the following steps:

1. Load the `SoundEffect` object via the content manager.
2. Create an instance of the sound effect.
3. Set volume, pitch, pan, and loop.
4. Play the sound.

The result should be the sound playing in a loop, one octave higher than the recorded effect, half the current system volume and entirely in the left channel. The code is as follows:

```
jumpSound = Content.Load<SoundEffect>("Jump");
jumpInstance = jumpSound.CreateInstance();
jumpInstance.Volume = 0.5f;
jumpInstance.Pitch = 1.0f;
jumpInstance.Pan = -1.0f;
jumpInstance.IsLooped = true;

jumpInstance.Play();
```

The instance also offers support for stopping, pausing, and resuming the sound, but these methods are self explanatory. The SoundEffectInstance object also has a State property that can be used to determine if the SoundEffectInstance object is playing, paused, or stopped.

Playing 3D sound

When playing sounds, for instance an explosion, it's nice that the sound of the explosion actually appears to be coming from the explosion. This can be done using 3D sound. The basic setup is very similar as using a SoundEffectInstance, because it has support for 3D sound. We just need some extra classes: an AudioEmitter and an AudioListener. The emitter represents the object that will cause the sound, for instance in case of an explosion, the bomb. The emitter will have the same position as the object that creates the sound. The listener represents the object that receives the sound. In case of a game, it would be the player, and thus have the same position. Both the emitter and the listener have a property called Forward; with the emitter, it defines the direction in which the sound should travel; with the listener, if defines the direction in which the listener is oriented. They both have properties for the position, the up vector and the velocity. The emitter also has a property to set the Doppler scale. The Doppler effect is the change in frequency of a sound we might observe caused by the speed difference between the emitter and the listener. Let's start with a demo. In this demo, we will assume the listener is positioned at the origin and the emitter will move.

Fields

We need to create several fields.

1. A sound effect
2. An instance of the sound affect

3. An emitter

4. A listener

The code is as follows:

```
SoundEffect explosionSound;
SoundEffectInstance explosionInstance;

AudioEmitter emitter = new AudioEmitter();
AudioListener listener = new AudioListener();
```

LoadContent

In the `LoadContent` method, we will create the sound effect and the instance and set it to loop. We will call the `Apply3D` method on the instance, passing the listener and the emitter as arguments. We need to do this before we call play for the first time, otherwise it won't be a 3D sound. Finally we call play on the instance.

```
explosionSound = Content.Load<SoundEffect>("Explosion");
explosionInstance = explosionSound.CreateInstance();
explosionInstance.IsLooped = true;

// Call Apply3D before the first play to make it a 3D sound.
explosionInstance.Apply3D(listener, emitter);

explosionInstance.Play();
```

Update

In the update, we will change the position of the emitter and apply the effects to the instance of our explosion. We will use a `sinus` function to move the emitter about all axes.

```
emitter.Position = new Vector3(
        (float)Math.Sin(gameTime.TotalGameTime.TotalSeconds),
        (float)Math.Sin(gameTime.TotalGameTime.TotalSeconds),
        (float)Math.Sin(gameTime.TotalGameTime.TotalSeconds));

explosionInstance.Apply3D(listener, emitter);
```

Result

When you press *F5* and the application launches, you will hear the explosion move around.

Playing a song

Sometimes you want to play a song instead of a sound, for instance background music for a game. The MediaPlayer class is a static class that exposes functionality to play songs. This class is also more advanced than the previous classes, in the sense that you can make it act like a true media player, and play, pause, resume, mute, repeat, shuffle, and so on. And of course, it is possible to play songs from the user's media library. But let's start simple. We can load a song the usual way, via the content manager. Note that we have to use a different processor, being the Song processor. Game Studio 4.0 selects a default processor based on file type, that is Song for MP3 files. After loading the song, we can play it using the media library:

```
Song song = game.Content.Load<Song>("MySong");
MediaPlayer.Play(song);
```

The previous code would work perfectly, but it has some issues. First of all, if we were to submit a game with this code to the Windows Phone Marketplace, it would fail. This is because we didn't check if the user was playing music. To resolve this, check if the game has control (and the user isn't playing music). If so, play the song, if not, ask for permission to play the song (this can be done via a popup for instance).

```
if (MediaPlayer.GameHasControl)
    MediaPlayer.Play(song);
else
    //AskForPermissionAndThenPlaySong
```

Note that MediaPlayer is a static class, so we don't have to instantiate it using new. If you want to stop the song that is currently playing, you can use MediaPlayer.Stop() method. The play method can play just one song, or an entire song collection. In the case of a collection, it would queue the entire collection and start playing the first song in the collection.

Now let's play a song from the user's media library. First we need to add a new field that will represent the media library. Call it library.

```
MediaLibrary library = new MediaLibrary();
```

In the `Initialize` method, we can check if the game has control, and if the library contains any songs. If so, we can play the first song from the library.

```
if (MediaPlayer.GameHasControl && library.Songs.Count > 0)
    MediaPlayer.Play(library.Songs[0]);
```

Note that when you exit the application, the song will keep playing, so we have to stop it ourselves. In the update, add the following code:

```
if (GamePad.GetState(PlayerIndex.One).Buttons.Back == ButtonState.
Pressed)
{
    if (MediaPlayer.GameHasControl)
        MediaPlayer.Stop();
    this.Exit();
}
```

If you run the game by pressing *F5*, you should hear the first song in your library.

The media player has lots more functionality, but most of it is self explanatory. Feel free to experiment with it.

Summary

In this chapter, we've covered the ways you can play sounds and music on a Windows Phone device to create a richer experience for your game, going from 2D sound to 3D sound and playing background music.

Now that we have covered all the basics, we can start by building a small framework in the next chapter. This includes a small scene graph, a level system, and implementing collision detection. We will then use this framework for our game.

6
Building a Basic Framework

In the previous chapters, we covered Sound, so now we understand all the basics. However, we still don't have a basic framework that allows us to build games in an ordered manner. So in this chapter, we will cover some concepts that will help us achieve just that. In this chapter we will cover:

- Scene graph
- Scene manager
- Collision detection
- Menus

Scene graph

A scene graph is often used in game development to link objects together. This link can be logical, for instance a sword can be seen as a part of the hero; but it can also be spatial: the sword moves along with the hero (assuming he doesn't drop it of course). A scene graph can be visualized as a system of nodes; each node can have a parent, siblings, and children. The position, rotation, and scale of a child will be relative to its parent. For instance, if our hero moves, the sword would also move, even though you don't change the position of the sword itself.

Implementation

We will update `GameObject2D` and `GameObject3D` so they implement this concept. Each object will hold a list of children and a reference to its parent (if a parent exists). Note that the implementation is very similar (if not almost identical) for `GameObject2D` and `GameObject3D`; therefore the code in this section will be the implementation of `GameObject2D`. We can find the implementation of `GameObject3D` in the code accompanying this chapter.

Fields

In the original `GameObject2D` class, we had three fields that were spatial, being the position, rotation, and scale of the object. Because we will be implementing a basic scene graph, we can delete these. Instead, we need to differentiate between local and world space. The local space of the object is the position, rotation, and scale we give it. The world position, rotation, and scale will be relative to its parents. Therefore, we need to create separate properties. We will also create a property called `PivotPoint`. This can be seen as an anchor point which you will rotate about. For instance, if we have a sphere, and we want to rotate it about our hero, we can use the pivot point. If we were to use the rotation, the object would rotate about its axis before translating; with the pivot point, we can translate first, then rotate, then translate again. Finally we will also create a matrix that will hold the world matrix of our object.

```
public Vector2 LocalPosition { get; set; }
public Vector2 WorldPosition { get; private set; }

public Vector2 LocalScale { get; set; }
public Vector2 WorldScale { get; private set; }

public float LocalRotation { get; set; }
public float WorldRotation { get; private set; }

public Vector2 PivotPoint { get; set; }

protected Matrix WorldMatrix;
```

Next we need a reference to our parent, which is of type `GameObject2D`, and we also need a list of children.

```
public GameObject2D Parent { get; set; }
public List<GameObject2D> Children { get; private set; }
```

Finally, we will add a property that defines if the object should be drawn before or after the 3D. A background should be drawn before, while a heads up display should be drawn after.

```
public bool DrawBefore3D { get; set; }
```

Constructor

In the constructor, we need to set the local and world scale to one, and initialize our list of children.

```
LocalScale = WorldScale = Vector2.One;
Children = new List<GameObject2D>();
CanDraw = true;
```

Methods

We added several methods to our `GameObject2D` that will enable us to manage the local position, rotation, and scale. Not all the code is copied in this chapter, because it's very straight forward, as illustrated in the following snippet:

```
public void Translate(Vector2 position)
{
    LocalPosition = position;
}
```

We also need to expose some behavior for adding and removing children.

```
public void AddChild(GameObject2D child)
{
    if (!Children.Contains(child))
    {
        Children.Add(child);
        child.Parent = this;
    }
}

public void RemoveChild(GameObject2D child)
{
    if (Children.Remove(child))
        child.Parent = null;
}
```

Beside that we also need to pass the `Initialize`, `LoadContent`, and `Draw` calls to our children. As the implementation is similar, only the `Initialize` method is illustrated in the following code:

```
public virtual void Initialize()
{
    Children.ForEach(child => child.Initialize());
}
```

Finally we have to update. This method is a lot trickier because we need to calculate the world position, rotation, and scale before updating our children. This is done in two parts. In the first part we need to calculate our final world matrix. This is fairly straight forward.

1. We translate to the negative of our pivot point.

2. Multiply by scale.

3. Rotate about the origin, or pivot point if set.

4. Translate to the local position.

5. If we have a parent, we translate with its pivot point, and then multiply with its world matrix (this will make sure our position is relative to our parent).

```
WorldMatrix =
    Matrix.CreateTranslation(new Vector3(-PivotPoint, 0)) *
    Matrix.CreateScale(new Vector3(LocalScale, 1)) *
    Matrix.CreateRotationZ(
        MathHelper.ToRadians(LocalRotation)) *
    Matrix.CreateTranslation(new Vector3(LocalPosition, 0));

if (Parent != null)
{
    WorldMatrix = Matrix.Multiply(WorldMatrix,
      Matrix.CreateTranslation(
        new Vector3(Parent.PivotPoint, 0))
      );
    WorldMatrix = Matrix.Multiply(WorldMatrix,
      Parent.WorldMatrix);
}
```

Now we have our final position, rotation, and scale. They are stored in a matrix, and now we have to get them out in order to set our world position, rotation, and scale properties. We can do this by calling Decompose on the matrix.

```
Vector3 pos, scale;
Quaternion rot;
if (!WorldMatrix.Decompose(out scale, out rot, out pos))
    Debug.WriteLine("Object2D Decompose World Matrix FAILED!");
```

One issue we have is that the rotation is a Quaternion. The problem is that we need a float. We can convert this by doing the following:

1. Transform the unit vector for the x axis with the quaternion. This will give us a direction.

2. Transform the direction to a rotation by calculating the angle. We can do this by using the Atan2 method.

3. If the resulting angle is a number, use it, otherwise we need to use 0.

```
var direction = Vector2.Transform(Vector2.UnitX, rot);
WorldRotation = (float)Math.Atan2(direction.Y, direction.X);
WorldRotation = float.IsNaN(WorldRotation) ? 0 :
            MathHelper.ToDegrees(WorldRotation);
```

4. Finally, we can set our world position and rotation, and update our children.

```
WorldPosition = new Vector2(pos.X, pos.Y);
WorldScale = new Vector2(scale.X, scale.Y);

Children.ForEach(child => child.Update(renderContext));
```

Using the code

That's it for the scene graph. Using the code is very simple, as we can see in the code example accompanying this book. For instance, our explosion sprite and rock sprite are children of our Rock2D class. If we would move the Rock2D class, the rock sprite and explosion sprite would move with it. We just need to set our pivot point correctly.

```
_rockSprite = new GameSprite("Game2D/Rock");
_rockSprite.PivotPoint = new Vector2(10, 25);
_rockSprite.CanDraw = false;
AddChild(_rockSprite);
```

Scene manager

So now we have a basic scene graph. The only problem is switching between scenes. If we want to switch between the 2D and 3D scene, we need to change a lot of code in our game class. And that's only with two scenes; games tend to have a lot more. It would be a lot simpler to be able to add multiple scenes to our game and just select an active one. It's time we did just that.

The GameScene

If we want to create a scene manager, we first need a class that will represent a scene.

Properties

Let us start by identifying the properties of a scene. A scene should have a name, along with a list of 2D game objects and a list of 3D game objects.

```
public string SceneName { get; private set; }
public List<GameObject2D> SceneObjects2D { get; private set; }
public List<GameObject3D> SceneObjects3D { get; private set; }
```

Constructor

The constructor will have one argument of type string, being the name of the scene. In the body, we will set the name, and create new containers for our game objects.

```
SceneName = name;
SceneObjects2D = new List<GameObject2D>();
SceneObjects3D = new List<GameObject3D>();
```

Methods

First of all, we will need methods for adding and removing game objects. This code is very similar to what we did in the scene graph. Note that we will have to write this code for 2D and 3D game objects. The following code is for 2D game objects. The overloaded methods for 3D are exactly the same, except the type of the scene object and the use of `SceneObjects3D`.

```
public void AddSceneObject(GameObject2D sceneObject)
{
    if (!SceneObjects2D.Contains(sceneObject))
    {
        sceneObject.Scene = this;
        SceneObjects2D.Add(sceneObject);
    }
}

public void RemoveSceneObject(GameObject2D sceneObject)
{
    if (SceneObjects2D.Remove(sceneObject))
    {
        sceneObject.Scene = null;
    }
}
```

Note that we are setting the `Scene` property of the game object. We will need to add this to the game objects, as it currently does not exist. We will also need to set the scene property in when adding and removing a child object.

```
// In GameObject2D and GameObject3D
private GameScene _scene;
public GameScene Scene
{
    get
    {
        if (_scene != null) return _scene;
        if (Parent != null) return Parent.Scene;
```

```
            return null;
    }

    set { _scene = value; }
}
```

Okay, almost there, we still need to patch though the `Initialize`, `LoadContent`, `Update`, `Draw2D`, and `Draw3D` methods to the game objects. Because the implementation is very similar, we can only see the `Initialize` and `Draw2D` in the following code snippet. Note that we only call the `Draw2D` method on the `game` object if the `DrawBefore3D` property is equal to the argument.

```
public virtual void Initialize()
{
    SceneObjects2D.ForEach(sceneObject =>
                    sceneObject.Initialize());
    SceneObjects3D.ForEach(sceneObject =>
                    sceneObject.Initialize());
}
public virtual void Draw2D(RenderContext renderContext, bool
drawBefore3D)
{
    SceneObjects2D.ForEach(obj =>
    {
        if (obj.DrawBefore3D == drawBefore3D)
            obj.Draw(renderContext);
    });
}
```

That's it for the `GameScene` class. Time to implement the `SceneManager`.

The SceneManager

So now we have a class, the `GameScene`, which can hold game objects and call all the appropriate methods. Now we need a class that can manage all the scenes and set the appropriate scene as active. We will make this class static, so we can access it from everywhere.

Properties

This class needs three properties: a list of scenes, the active scene, and the render context. The scene manager will manage the render context and pass it to the active scene when needed.

```
public static List<GameScene> GameScenes {get; private set;}
public static GameScene ActiveScene {get; private set;}
public static RenderContext RenderContext {get; private set;}
```

Constructor

In the constructor, we need to initialize our list of game scenes and the render context. We also need to set the default camera for the render context, and thus **add** a property for our camera to the render context.

```
GameScenes = new List<GameScene>();
RenderContext = new RenderContext();
//Default Camera
RenderContext.Camera = new BaseCamera();
```

Managing the scenes

We will need methods for adding and removing game scenes. These are very straight forward and just add items to the scene collection. We will also need to be able to set the active scene. We can do this by searching through our collection and see if we have a scene that has the same name as the argument. If so, we can set it as the active scene.

```
public static void AddGameScene(GameScene gameScene)
{
    if (!GameScenes.Contains(gameScene))
        GameScenes.Add(gameScene);
}

public static void RemoveGameScene(GameScene gameScene)
{
    GameScenes.Remove(gameScene);

    if (ActiveScene == gameScene) ActiveScene = null;
}

public static bool SetActiveScene(string name)
{
    var chosenScene = GameScenes. FirstOrDefault (
      scene => scene.SceneName.Equals(name));

    if (chosenScene != null)
    {
        ActiveScene = chosenScene;
    }

    return chosenScene != null;
}
```

Initialize and LoadContent

These methods are very simple, and we just pass the method call to the game scenes as illustrated in the following code:

```
public static void Initialize()
{
    GameScenes.ForEach(scene => scene.Initialize());
}
```

Update and Draw

The `Update` and `Draw` method are only called on the active scene, if we currently have an active scene. In the update, we will also set the game time of our render context object.

```
public static void Update(GameTime gameTime)
{
    if (ActiveScene != null)
    {
        RenderContext.GameTime = gameTime;
        ActiveScene.Update(RenderContext);
    }
}
```

In the `Draw` method, we will first draw our 2D items that need to be drawn before the 3D (for example, the background), reset the render states, draw the 3D, and finally draw the 2D items that have to be drawn after the 3D (for example, the heads up display).

```
if (ActiveScene != null)
{
    //2D Before 3D
    RenderContext.SpriteBatch.Begin();
    ActiveScene.Draw2D(RenderContext, true);
    RenderContext.SpriteBatch.End();

    //DRAW 3D
    //Reset Renderstate
    RenderContext.GraphicsDevice.BlendState =
                    BlendState.Opaque;
    RenderContext.GraphicsDevice.DepthStencilState =
                    DepthStencilState.Default;
    RenderContext.GraphicsDevice.SamplerStates[0] =
                    SamplerState.LinearWrap;
```

```
ActiveScene.Draw3D(RenderContext);

//2D After 3D
RenderContext.SpriteBatch.Begin();
ActiveScene.Draw2D(RenderContext, false);
RenderContext.SpriteBatch.End();
}
```

Creating scenes

Now that we have everything set up, we can create some scenes. Let's start by creating a Game2D scene that will hold the code for our 2D game. The 3D game will then be similar.

We need to create a class that inherits from GameScene and has three fields: our background, hero, and enemy. In the constructor, we call the constructor of the base class and pass a name. We also need to initialize our background, hero, and enemy and add them to the list of scene objects.

```
class Game2D : GameScene
{
    private GameSprite _background;
    private Hero2D _hero;
    private Enemy2D _enemy;

    public Game2D() : base("Game2D")
    {
        _background = new GameSprite("Game2D/BackGround");
        AddSceneObject(_background);

        _hero = new Hero2D();
        AddSceneObject(_hero);

        _enemy = new Enemy2D();
        AddSceneObject(_enemy);
    }
}
```

Updating the main game

We can start by deleting all the code we've written in the main game and only leave the default code in there.

Initialize

In the `initialize` method, we need to perform the following steps:

1. Set the graphics device property of our render context.
2. Add the game scenes.
3. Set the active scene.
4. Initialize the scene manager.

    Note that the following code assumes we also have a `Game3D` scene.

    ```
    SceneManager.RenderContext.GraphicsDevice =
                                graphics.GraphicsDevice;

    SceneManager.AddGameScene(new Game2D());
    SceneManager.AddGameScene(new Game3D());

    SceneManager.SetActiveScene("Game2D");
    SceneManager.Initialize();
    ```

LoadContent

In the `LoadContent` method, we need to set the `SpriteBatch` property of our render context and call `LoadContent` method on our scene manager.

```
SceneManager.RenderContext.SpriteBatch = spriteBatch;
SceneManager.LoadContent(Content);
```

Update and Draw

In these methods, we need to pass the appropriate method call to our scene manager, as illustrated in the following code:

```
SceneManager.Update(gameTime);
```

Result

As a result, we can switch between multiple scenes. The complete code accompanies this chapter.

Collision

Now we will implement collision, and by collision we actually mean collision detection. We will detect whether two objects are currently colliding with each other. We can then create appropriate actions. Not that we will not actually implement the physical collision (for instance a car hitting the wall). If we want to do this, we should use a physics engine.

We will make a difference between 2D collision and 3D collision. When testing for collision of two 2D game objects, we use rectangles. This rectangle surrounds the object, and we can then check whether these rectangles intersect with each other. Note that if you have a cross for instance, the bounding rectangle will be too big for the object, but for our intended purposes, a rectangle will do just fine.

3D collision is very similar to 2D collision; the only difference is that we will use the `BoundingBox` class instead of the `Rectangle` class. All the steps are the same as with 2D collision, but we make use of 3D coordinates. This code comes with the chapter, but the following code is for the 2D implementation.

The extension method

Before we start updating `GameObject2D`, we need to write an extension method. An extension method is a static method (in a static class), where the first argument has `this` before the type name. This will make sure we can use the method as if it was part of the class. In our case, we want to add the `Update` method to the `Rectangle` class. But because this class is in the XNA framework and we can't access it, we need to write an extension method.

```
public static Rectangle Update(this Rectangle rectangle, Matrix
transform)
```

In this extension method, we will transform our rectangle with the world matrix, thus moving it with our object. The problem is our object can be rotated, and this rotation can change the size of the rectangle. So we need to calculate the smallest possible rectangle by looping over all corners and selecting the minimum and maximum. The result is a new, transformed, rectangle.

```
var corners = new Vector2[]
{
    new Vector2(rectangle.Left,rectangle.Top),
    new Vector2(rectangle.Right,rectangle.Bottom),
    new Vector2(rectangle.Left,rectangle.Bottom),
    new Vector2(rectangle.Right,rectangle.Top)
};
var transformedCorners = new Vector2[corners.Length];
```

```
Vector2.Transform(corners, ref transform, transformedCorners);

var newMin = new Vector3(float.MaxValue);
var newMax = new Vector3(float.MinValue);

foreach (var corner in transformedCorners)
{
    newMin.X = Math.Min(newMin.X, corner.X);
    newMin.Y = Math.Min(newMin.Y, corner.Y);

    newMax.X = Math.Max(newMax.X, corner.X);
    newMax.Y = Math.Max(newMax.Y, corner.Y);
}

int width = (int)(newMax.X - newMin.X);
int height = (int)(newMax.Y - newMin.Y);
return new Rectangle((int)newMin.X, (int)newMin.Y,
            width, height);
```

Updating GameObject2D

First, we need to add some fields and properties. We will have one private field: our original rectangle. We will also have one extra property, being our rectangle that has been transformed to world space. Note that these are both `Nullable`, as we don't need a bounding rectangle for every object.

```
private Rectangle? _relativeBoundingRect;
public Rectangle? BoundingRect { get; protected set; }
```

Next we can add methods to create a bounding rectangle, using a width, height, and offset. We will also create a method that tests for collision called `HitTest`. This method will test the object and all children for collision using the `Intersect` method of a rectangle.

```
public void CreateBoundingRect(int width, int height, Vector2 offset)
{
    _relativeBoundingRect = new Rectangle(0, 0, width +
            (int)offset.X, height + (int)offset.Y);
    BoundingRect = _relativeBoundingRect;
}

public void CreateBoundingRect(int width, int height)
{
    CreateBoundingRect(width, height, Vector2.Zero);
```

```
    }

    public bool HitTest(GameObject2D gameObj)
    {
        if (!gameObj.BoundingRect.HasValue) return false;
        if (BoundingRect.HasValue &&
              BoundingRect.Value.Intersects(
                gameObj.BoundingRect.Value)
              ) return true;

        return Children.FirstOrDefault(child =>
                child.HitTest(gameObj)) != null;
    }
```

Finally, we need to update our bounding rectangle each frame, using the extension method we created previously.

```
if (_relativeBoundingRect.HasValue)
    BoundingRect =
      _relativeBoundingRect.Value.Update(WorldMatrix);
```

Updating Hero2D

If we want to add a bounding rectangle to our hero, we can do this in the `Initialize` method.

```
_heroSprite.CreateBoundingRect(32, 39, Vector2.Zero);
```

Testing for collisions

If we want to test for collisions, we can call the `HitTest` on a certain object passing the object we want to test against as argument.

```
if (_hero.HitTest(_otherObject))
    Debug.WriteLine("We have collision");
```

Result

We now have the possibility to add a `Rectangle` to 2D game objects, and a `BoundingBox` to 3D game objects. This allows us to do collision. We will need this in our game, and also in the next part where we will be drawing menus. Note that in the code that comes with this chapter, we've also added the possibility to draw the `Rectangle` and `BoundingBox`, as this is handy for debugging purposes. But as this is beyond the scope of this book, we won't explain the code here.

Note that we added two extra scenes in the demo code, one for 2D collision and on for 3D collision.

Menus

It's time we made some menus. If we want menus, we need buttons to press.
But before we make the buttons, we need to perform the following steps:

1. Because a button uses touch to determine if it's being pressed, we need to
   add the current touch state to the render context so all objects have the latest
   touch state. We do this by adding an extra property to the render context and
   by setting the latest touch state in the Update method of the scene manager.

   ```
   // Extra property of the render context
   public TouchCollection TouchPanelState { get; set; }

   // Update the TouchPanelState in the
   // Update of the Scene Manager
   RenderContext.TouchPanelState = TouchPanel.GetState();
   ```

2. Add an extra HitTest method to our GameObject2D. This because touch
   returns a point instead of a rectangle. We can check if a point is in a rectangle
   by using the Contains method. Note that we use an extra argument that
   specifies whether we want to test all the children. This is not always the case,
   as you will see in the menu scene, where we will add buttons as children of
   other buttons, but do not want to test for collision with the child.

   ```
   public bool HitTest(Vector2 position, bool includechildren)
   {
       if (BoundingRect.HasValue &&
           BoundingRect.Value.Contains(
               (int)position.X, (int)position.Y)
           ) return true;

       if (includechildren)
           return Children.FirstOrDefault(
               child => child.HitTest(position, includechildren))
               != null;
       return false;
   }
   ```

The button

Visually, our button will be an image. Our button also has several actions one could do. We can click it, enter it, and leave it. That's why our button will have three events: OnClick, OnEnter, and OnLeave. We will then be able to subscribe to this event from another class and determine what action should be performed when the event is called.

Let's start by creating a new class called GameButton that inherits from GameSprite class.

```
public class GameButton : GameSprite
```

Fields and events

Our class will have five fields: one that determines if our button is a sprite sheet (with a different texture to draw when entered, two fields of type Rectangle that represent the normal draw rectangle and the pressed draw rectangle, a Boolean that determines if the button is currently pressed and an integer that contains the current touch id (if no touch ID is available this will be -1).

```
private bool _isSpriteSheet;
private Rectangle? _normalRect, _pressedRect;
private bool _isPressed;
private int _touchId;
```

The class will also three events as explained in the previous code.

```
public event Action OnClick;
public event Action OnEnter;
public event Action OnLeave;
```

Constructor

The constructor is very straight forward. We have two arguments, one being the asset file, and one that specifies if our button uses a sprite sheet or not.

```
public GameButton(string assetFile, bool isSpriteSheet) :
    base(assetFile)
{
    _isSpriteSheet = isSpriteSheet;
}
```

LoadContent

In this method, we will create our bounding rectangle and calculate our draw rectangles. If we use a sprite sheet, we assume the top half is the normal state, and the bottom half is the pressed state.

```
//Set Dimensions after the button texture is loaded, otherwise //we
can't extract the width and height
if (_isSpriteSheet)
{
    CreateBoundingRect((int)Width, (int)Height / 2);
    _normalRect = new Rectangle(0, 0,
                (int)Width, (int)(Height / 2f));

    _pressedRect = new Rectangle(0, (int)(Height / 2f),
                (int)Width, (int)(Height / 2f));
}
else CreateBoundingRect((int)Width, (int)Height);
```

Update

In the update, we'll see if we currently pressed, released, or entered the button, and call the appropriate event handlers. The logic is as follows:

1. If we didn't press the button in the previous frame, we are going to set the draw rectangle to default, and loop over all touch locations. If we find one that has a hit, we will raise the OnEnter event and set the appropriate states.

2. If we did have a press in the previous frame, we are going to perform a hit test on the touch location with the id of the previous frame. If it returns a touch location, we will perform a hit test. If that test was positive or we didn't have a touch location, we have left the button and should raise OnLeave. If we had a touch location that didn't return a positive hit test and the state is set to released, we raise the OnClick event.

```
var touchStates = renderContext.TouchPanelState;
if (!_isPressed)
{
    DrawRect = _normalRect;

    foreach (var touchLoc in touchStates)
    {
        if (HitTest(touchLoc.Position, false))
        {
            _isPressed = true;
            _touchId = touchLoc.Id;
```

```
                    //ENTERED
                    if (OnEnter != null) OnEnter();
                    DrawRect = _pressedRect;
                    break;
                }
            }
        }
        else
        {
            var touchLoc = touchStates.FirstOrDefault(
              tLocation => tLocation.Id == _touchId);

            if (touchLoc == null
              || !HitTest(touchLoc.Position, false))
            {
                _touchId = -1;
                _isPressed = false;
                //LEFT
                if (OnLeave != null) OnLeave();
            }
            else
            {
                if (touchLoc.State == TouchLocationState.Released)
                {
                    _touchId = -1;
                    _isPressed = false;
                    //CLICKED
                    if (OnClick != null) OnClick();
                }
            }
        }
    }
```

The menu scene

Finally, we can create the new menu scene. This is a normal game scene, and we
name it Menu. In the Initialize method, we can create all the buttons we want.
In the following example, we create a new button, translate it, scale it, set the pivot
point and add an event handler for the clicked event.

```
GameButton btnGame2D = new GameButton("Buttons/Scene2DButton",
                          true);

btnGame2D.Translate(TouchPanel.DisplayWidth / 2f,
          TouchPanel.DisplayHeight / 2f - 150);
btnGame2D.PivotPoint = new Vector2(62, 20);
```

```
btnGame2D.Scale(2, 2);
btnGame2D.OnClick += Game2D_OnClick;
AddSceneObject(btnGame2D);
```

The event handler itself is pretty simple, as it will only set the appropriate scene as active.

```
private void Game2D_OnClick()
{
    SceneManager.SetActiveScene("Game2D");
}
```

We can then add buttons for all the scenes you want in a similar manner. We can even position them relatively simply by adding them as a child to the previous button, as illustrated in the attached example.

Finally, we can also update our main game so it returns to the menu when the back button is pressed, and it only exits when the back button is pressed when inside the menu.

```
if (GamePad.GetState(PlayerIndex.One).Buttons.Back == ButtonState.
Pressed)
{
    if (SceneManager.ActiveScene.SceneName == "Menu") Exit();
    else SceneManager.SetActiveScene("Menu");
}
```

Result

The result is a menu we can use to navigate through our scenes, as illustrated in the following code snippet:

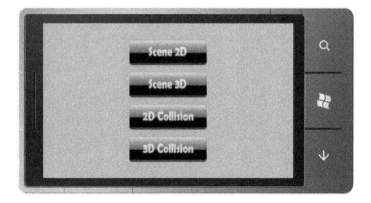

Summary

In this chapter, we've built a basic framework that will help us to build games without getting cluttered code, and covered some extra aspects such as collision and menus.

Now that everything is ready for us to begin, let's build a game in the next chapter!

7
Building a Game

In the previous chapter, we covered the build of a basic framework, so now we have all the pieces in place to start building a game. We will build the game in several steps:

- Game concept
- Menu scene
- Level scene

Game concept

Before we can start building a game, we need a game concept. It's very important that you know what you want to create before even writing one line of code. Let's have a look at our game concept. Our game is about a running vampire who can slide, jump, or deflect projectiles by lifting his shield up. These actions are useless if they have no purpose. So we will add some obstacles, this way our hero can use his actions to get around these obstacles.

The game will contain three mechanics to keep things fun and interesting:

- Our hero runs from the left-hand side to the right-hand side, avoiding obstacles using his actions:
  - ° Sliding under a swinging iron ball
  - ° Jumping over rusty spikes
  - ° Raising the shield to deflect falling rocks

- Each action will be represented by a button on the **Head-up display** (HUD), but they will swap places after being pressed. This way it's more challenging to select the appropriate action.

- We will increase the game speed each time we pass a certain amount of obstacles.

The goal is simple—don't get hit by one of the obstacles, otherwise it is game over!

With these three game mechanics, we are able to build a simple but interesting game. The next screenshot gives us a sneak peak of the game:

Menu scene

We will start this demo from a fresh project that you can find in the `StartFiles` folder. This project already contains all the assets and a basic folder setup that will help us organize our game files.

We will create a simple menu with two buttons, one to start the game and another one to exit the game. Let's start by creating a new class called `MenuScene` that inherits from `GameScene`.

```
public class MenuScene :GameScene
```

Fields

Our class will have four fields: a background, two buttons, and a `SoundEffect` class.

```
private GameSprite _background;
private GameButton _startButton;
private GameButton _exitButton;
private Song _backgroundMusic;
```

Constructor

The constructor remains empty but we need to pass the name of this scene to the base class.

```
public MenuScene():base("Menu"){}
```

Initialize

In this method, we will initialize the background and the buttons. The `PivotPoint` property of the buttons is set at the top-middle; this will make it easy to position them on the middle of the screen. We also add an event handler to the `OnClick` event of the buttons. The event handlers are pretty simple. A click on the start button will set the `Level` scene active and a click on the exit button will exit the game.

```
_background = new GameSprite("Sprites\\MenuBackground");
AddSceneObject(_background);

_startButton = new GameButton("Sprites\\StartButton", true);
_startButton.PivotPoint = new Vector2(162, 0);
_startButton.Translate(400, 150);
_startButton.OnClick += () => SceneManager.SetActiveScene("Level");
AddSceneObject(_startButton);

_exitButton = new GameButton("Sprites\\ExitButton", true);
_exitButton.PivotPoint = new Vector2(162, 0);
_exitButton.Translate(400, 250);
_exitButton.OnClick += () => SceneManager.MainGame.Exit();
AddSceneObject(_exitButton);
```

LoadContent

Before we can play the music, we need to load it. We use the content manager to load the `Song` object (make sure that the asset's processor is set to `Song`). As seen in *Chapter 5, Sound* we need the static `MediaPlayer` class to play a sound. And because we want to loop this sound, we also set `MediaPlayer.IsRepeating` to `true`.

```
_backgroundMusic = contentManager.Load<Song>("BackgroundMusic");
MediaPlayer.IsRepeating = true;
MediaPlayer.Play(_backgroundMusic);
```

The last thing we need to do is to add this menu scene to the `SceneManager` class. This is done in the `Initialize` method of the `MainGame` class.

```
SceneManager.AddGameScene(new MenuScene());
SceneManager.SetActiveScene("Menu");
```

That's all for the menu scene, when you run the game a menu should pop up. Note that clicking on the **Start** button does nothing, that's because the level scene doesn't exist at the moment.

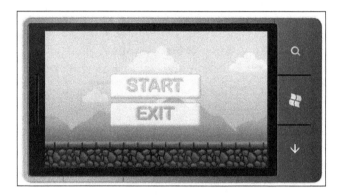

Level Scene

The level scene is the heart of the game. This scene will manage all the different game objects and interactions.

Prerequisites

One of our game mechanics is the game speed, and it's important that every object can retrieve the current game speed. That's why we need to add two extra fields to the `RenderContext` class, one for the current game speed and another one for the initial game speed.

```
public float GameSpeed { get; set; }
public float InitialGameSpeed { get; set; }
```

Level Scene

Create a new class called `LevelScene` that inherits from `GameScene`.

```
public class LevelScene:GameScene
```

In the constructor, you need to pass the scene name to the base class, name it "Level".

```
public LevelScene():base("Level"){}
```

We also need to add this GameScene to the SceneManager class in the Initialize method of our MainGame class.

```
SceneManager.AddGameScene(new LevelScene());
```

That's all we can do at the moment. Let's create some game objects so we can fill up this level scene.

Background

To give our game some extra depth, we will use a layered background. Several layers, scrolling at a different speed will provide us with an extra sense of depth. However, unlike three-dimensional objects, our background isn't affected by the camera movement because it's completely two-dimensional. That's why we will have to scroll the layers manually. Create a new class called Background that inherits from GameObjects2D.

```
public class Background:GameObject2D
```

Fields

The background contains five different layers:

- Front clouds layer (closest layer)
- Middle clouds layer
- Mountains layer
- Back clouds layer
- Air layer (blue sky and farthest layer)

The next screenshot gives us an impression of how it will look like. All the layers except for the air layer will scroll horizontally with a different speed; a percentage of the actual game speed:

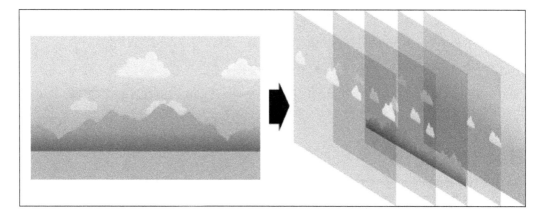

We will create a field of type GameSprite for each layer and also a const float field for each scrolling layer that we will use to calculate the final layer speed based on the actual game speed.

```
private GameSprite _air;

private const float MOUNTAINS_SPEED = 0.4f;
private GameSprite _mountains;

private const float CLOUDS_FRONT_SPEED = 0.7f;
private GameSprite _cloudsFront;

private const float CLOUDS_MIDDLE_SPEED = 0.5f;
private GameSprite _cloudsMiddle;

private const float CLOUDS_BACK_SPEED = 0.3f;
private GameSprite _cloudsBack;
```

Initialize

We need to initialize all the GameSprite objects and add them to the child list GameObject2D. The order of adding these layers is very important; this is also the order of drawing. We start with initializing and adding the air layer.

```
_air = new GameSprite("Sprites\\Background_Air");
AddChild(_air);
```

Do the same for the `_cloudsBack`, `_mountains`, `_cloudsMiddle`, and `_cloudsFront` layers.

Update

In the `Update` method, we need to move each layer with a certain speed to obtain the scrolling effect. Let's have a look at the logic to scroll the mountain layer:

1. We start with defining the actual layer speed based on the current game speed and the layer speed percent (`gameSpeed*MOUNTAIN_SPEED`). This gives us the `objectSpeed` variable.

2. Multiply the `objectSpeed` variable with the `ElapsedGameTime`. `TotalSeconds` property to ensure a frame rate independent behaviour.

3. The hero will run from the left-hand side to the right-hand, so our background needs to scroll from the right-hand side to the left-hand side. That's why we need to subtract the value of `objectSpeed` from `_mountains`. `LocalPosition.X`.

4. If the `objectPosX` variable is smaller than `-800`, so we know that we reached the end of the image (the image has a width of 1600 px, so we can only move it -800 px). As we move it 800 px to the right-hand side, there will be no visual difference because the images are tileable.

5. The last step is translating the image itself with the new X position.

```
//Mountains Position
var objectSpeed = renderContext.GameSpeed * MOUNTAINS_SPEED;
objectSpeed *= (float)renderContext.GameTime.ElapsedGameTime.
TotalSeconds;

var objectPosX = _mountains.LocalPosition.X - objectSpeed;

if (objectPosX < -800)
    objectPosX += 800;

_mountains.Translate(objectPosX, 225);
```

6. Now we need to do the same for the other layers. The logic is the same as earlier except for two parameters (layer speed percentage, y-position):

   ○ Front clouds position (`CLOUDS_FRONT_SPEED`, y-position: 25)

   ○ Middle clouds position (`CLOUDS_MIDDLE_SPEED`, y-position: 130)

   ○ Back Clouds Position (`CLOUDS_BACK_SPEED`, y-position: 200)

Scene implementation

Our `Background` class is ready and can be implemented in the `LevelScene` class. First of all, we need to add a new field in the `LevelScene` class.

```
private Background _background;
```

In the `Initialize` method of `LevelScene` class, we will initialize our object and add it to the scene. We need to make sure that our background is drawn before we draw any three-dimensional content, otherwise the background will be in front of the three-dimensional content. And also give the `RenderContext.GameSpeed` value a temporary fixed value, that way we can see the background actually scrolling.

```
SceneManager.RenderContext.GameSpeed = 100;

_background = new Background();
_background.DrawBefore3D = true;
AddSceneObject(_background);
```

When we run the game and press **Start**, we can see our background with the scrolling layers. The fact that they are scrolling with a different speed gives us the impression of depth.

Path

Our hero needs something to walk on, some kind of a path. Because the hero keeps walking to the right-hand side, we need an infinite path. We can achieve this by breaking the path up in several parts that move themselves to the front of the path when they are too far behind. The following screenshot gives us an idea of such a system:

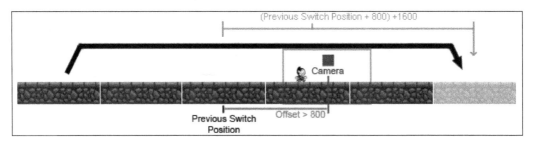

7. Create a new class called `Path` that inherits from `GameObject3D`.

    ```
    public class Path : GameObject3D
    ```

Fields

Our `Path` class has four fields:

- `_pathParts`: This is an array of type `GameModel` that contains five path models

- `_tailPartIndex`: This is an integer to store the index of the tail part

- `_prevSwitchPosition`: This is the last x-position when we switched a part

- `GROUND_POS`: This value is the top position of the path, which will be used in other classes too, that's why it's public

```
private GameModel[] _pathParts = new GameModel[5];
private int _tailPartIndex;
private float _prevSwitchPosition;
public const int GROUND_POS = -147;
```

Initialize

We will use a `for` loop to iterate the array, initialize position, and add each model. The model has a width of 800 units. So, we will place the first part at `-1600` and the second one at `-800`. The height of the model is `93` units, with its pivot point located at the bottom, we need to subtract the height from the `GROUND_POS` constant to make sure that the top of the path is located at `GROUND_POS`.

```
for (var i = 0; i < _pathParts.Length; ++i )
{
    _pathParts[i] = new GameModel("Models\\Path");
    _pathParts[i].Translate(-1600 + (800 * i), GROUND_POS - 93,
-100);
    AddChild(_pathParts[i]);
}
```

Update

In the `Update` method, we will move the end part of the path to the front of the path. We only need to do this when we moved more than or equal to 800 units since the last time we moved a part.

1. The camera's x-position subtracted by the `_prevSwitchPosition` field gives us the offset since the last time we switched a part. If this value is bigger than or equal to 800, we know that we need to switch a part.

2. Increase the `_prevSwitchPosition` field by `800`. This way we reset the offset.

3. Store the current local position of the tail part.

4. Change the x-component of the position, so the part is located at the beginning of the path.

5. Translate the part with the new position.

6. Increase the `_tailPartIndex` field. Using the modulo operator ensures that the value stays between [0, `_pathParts.Length`].

```
if (renderContext.Camera.LocalPosition.X - _prevSwitchPosition >=
800)
{
    _prevSwitchPosition += 800;

    var tailPos = _pathParts[_tailPartIndex].LocalPosition;
    tailPos = new Vector3(_prevSwitchPosition + 1600, tailPos.Y,
tailPos.Z);
    _pathParts[_tailPartIndex].Translate(tailPos);

    _tailPartIndex = (_tailPartIndex+1)%_pathParts.Length;
}
```

Scene implementation

Our `Path` class is ready and can be implemented in the `LevelScene` class. First of all, we need to add a new field in the `LevelScene` class.

```
private Path _path;
```

In the `Initialize` method of `LevelScene` class, we will initialize our object and add it to the scene.

```
_path = new Path();
AddSceneObject(_path);
```

Scene Camera

The path will only move when the camera moves, in contrast to the background where we did the scrolling part ourselves. The `SceneManager` class will create a `BaseCamera` object by default and store it in the `RenderContext.Camera` field. For now, we will use this default camera and later on we will create a new one. We need to add it to the scene to make it functional; we do that in the `Initialize` method of `LevelScene`.

```
AddSceneObject(SceneManager.RenderContext.Camera);
```

The last thing we need to do is move the camera each frame based on the game speed. We do that in the `Update` method of `LevelScene`:

```
//CAMERA MOVEMENT
var camPos = renderContext.Camera.LocalPosition;
camPos += new Vector3(renderContext.GameSpeed*(float) renderContext.
GameTime.ElapsedGameTime.TotalSeconds, 0, 0);
renderContext.Camera.Translate(camPos);
```

When we run the game and press **Start**, we can see our infinite path moving.

Buttons Controller

We need a way to trigger the hero's actions, which we can do with buttons. Each action will have its own button. Three buttons in total: one for sliding, one for jumping, and a last one to lift his shield. The button controller will limit us to pressing one button at a time. The buttons will also switch places when one of them is released, that's one of our game mechanics that makes the game more interesting. Create a new class called `ButtonsController` that inherits from `GameObject2D`.

```
public class ButtonsController:GameObject2D
```

Fields and properties

The buttons are stored in an array of `GameButton` instead of creating an individual field for each button. We can also easily iterate an array and prevent the duplication of code when we want to perform the same action on each button. There is also an array of `booleans` that indicates the state of the button. We also need to be able to force the release of a button, even if the player is still pressing it, that's why we have a second array of `booleans`. Both arrays of `booleans` are static, because we need to use them in a static method or property. There are also two fields to help us randomize the buttons inside a method called `RandomizeButtons`, a list of `GameButton`, and a field of type `Random`, our random generator. Then we also have three properties to retrieve the pressed state of a certain button. These three properties are also static, so we can access these properties in every class.

```
private GameButton[] _buttons = new GameButton[3];
private static bool[] _buttonsPressed = new bool[3];
private static bool[] _forcedRelease = new bool[3];

private static List<GameButton> _tempButtonList =
new List<GameButton>();
private static Random _random = new Random();

public static bool JumpPressed { get { return _buttonsPressed[0]; } }
```

```
public static bool SlidePressed { get { return _buttonsPressed[1]; } }
public static bool ShieldPressed { get { return _buttonsPressed[2]; }
}
```

Initialize

In the initialize method, we will initialize and add our buttons to the derived GameObject2D class. After this is done, we need to call the RandomizeButtons method; it doesn't exist at the moment but we will create it shortly.

```
_buttons[0] = new GameButton("Sprites\\JumpButton", true);
AddChild(_buttons[0]);

_buttons[1] = new GameButton("Sprites\\SlideButton", true);
AddChild(_buttons[1]);

_buttons[2] = new GameButton("Sprites\\ShieldButton", true);
AddChild(_buttons[2]);

RandomizeButtons();
```

RandomizeButtons method

This method will switch the buttons from place. The order is determined by a random generator.

1. Clear the _tempButtonList method and fill it up with the content of _buttons using the _tempButtonList.AddRange method.
2. Create a local variables to store the iteration count.
3. Iterate the list as long as it's not empty.
4. Use _random to pick a random index between [0, tempButtonList.Count].
5. Translate the button at that index using the iterations variable to determine the height.
6. Remove the object at that index from the list.
7. Increase the iteration count.

```
private void RandomizeButtons()
{
_tempButtonList.Clear();
_tempButtonList.AddRange(_buttons);
var iterations = 0;

while(_tempButtonList.Count>0)
```

```
{
var index = _random.Next(0, _tempButtonList.Count);
_tempButtonList[index].Translate(0,160*iterations);
_tempButtonList.RemoveAt(index);
++iterations;
}
}
```

Update

In the `Update` method, we will check the button's state and based on that, we set the corresponding `Boolean` in the `_buttonsPressed` array.

1. Iterate the `_buttons` array using a `for` loop.

2. If one of the buttons stored in the array is pressed and no other buttons are pressed, we set the corresponding `_buttonsPressed` `Boolean` to `true` except when the corresponding `_forcedRelease` `Boolean` is `false`.

3. Else if the button is not pressed but the corresponding `_buttonsPressed` or `_forcedRelease` `Boolean` is `true`, we know that the button is released. Reset all the corresponding states to `false` and call the `RadomizeButtons` method.

4. Otherwise, we set the corresponding `_buttonsPressed` `Boolean` to `false`.

```
for (var i = 0; i < _buttons.Length; ++i )
{
if (_buttons[i].IsPressed && (!JumpPressed || !SlidePressed ||
!ShieldPressed))
{
if(!_forcedRelease[i])_buttonsPressed[i] = true;
}
else if (!_buttons[i].IsPressed && (_buttonsPressed[i] || _
forcedRelease[i]))
{
_buttonsPressed[i] = false;
_forcedRelease[i] = false;
RandomizeButtons();
}
else _buttonsPressed[i] = false;
}
```

ForceButtonRelease method

With this method we can force a button release. The method has one argument, which is the index of the button we want to release. If the corresponding _ buttonsPressed Boolean is true, we set it to false and set the corresponding _forceRelease Boolean to true. Visually, the button will still be pressed but its corresponding _buttonsPressed Boolean will be false. This method is static, so it can be called from any class.

```
public static void ForceButtonRelease(int buttonIndex)
{
    if (_buttonsPressed[buttonIndex])
    {
        _buttonsPressed[buttonIndex] = false;
        _forcedRelease[buttonIndex] = true;
    }
}
```

Scene implementation

Our ButtonsController class is ready and can be implemented in the LevelScene class. First of all, we need to add a new field in the LevelScene class.

```
private ButtonsController _buttonsController;
```

In the Initialize method of LevelScene, we will initialize our object and add it to the scene.

```
_buttonsController = new ButtonsController();
AddSceneObject(_buttonsController);
```

When we run the game and press **Start**, we can see our three buttons. When we press one of the buttons and release it, the buttons switch places.

Hero

Our hero will run from the left-hand side to the right-hand side, and is always moving. He's also able to perform some actions, such as jumping, sliding, or lifting his shield. To manage all these actions, we will implement a state machine. This way, our code stays simple and clean. Let us start by creating a new class called Hero that inherits from GameObject3D.

```
public class Hero : GameObject3D
```

Fields and properties

To keep things clean and readable, we will create an enumeration that contains all the possible states of the hero.

```
public enum HeroAction
{
    Run,
    Shield,
    Jump,
    Slide,
    Die,
    None
}
```

The jump state needs a little bit more attention than the other states, because this is the only state where we need to add some extra movement to the hero. And in this game, it's also possible to let the hero hover for some time before gravity does its thing. There are three fields to control the jump state: _jumpTimer tracks the amount of time the hero is hovering, JUMP_TIMEOUT indicates the maximum time the hero can hover, and JUMP_SPEED indicates the initial speed when the hero jumps.

```
private float _jumpTimer;
private const float JUMP_TIMEOUT = 2.0f;
private const float JUMP_SPEED = 150.0f;
```

The other fields are pretty straight forward, except for the WorldPos property. Some objects such as the enemy, for example, need to know the current position of the hero. And that's why we added this property; the only thing it does is returning the WorldPosition of _model.

```
private GameAnimatedModel _model;
private Vector2 _velocity;
public HeroAction CurrentAction { get; private set; }
public Vector3 WorldPos { get{return _model.WorldPosition;} }
```

Initialize

In the initialize method, we need to initialize, position, and scale our _model object, and after that we add it to the derived GameObject3D class. For debugging purpose, we set DrawBoundingBox to true and when everything works, we can set it to false.

```
_model = new GameAnimatedModel("Models\\Hero");
_model.Translate(0, Path.GROUND_POS , -100);
_model.Scale(new Vector3(1.5f));
AddChild(_model);
```

```
DrawBoundingBox = true;
CurrentAction = HeroAction.None;
```

SetHeroAction method

The SetHeroAction method has one argument, that is, a HeroAction object. It does what the method name says; it sets the CurrentAction object to the new HeroAction object that we get as a parameter.

1. First we check if the new action isn't already set as CurrentAction.

2. Rotate the model to 90 degrees. This is done because the Die state will reset the rotation and this way we are sure that the model is rotated correctly.

3. Using a switch case, we change the model's animation and change the bounding box dimensions if needed. The Die state will also set the model back to its initial y-position and reset the current velocity.

4. Set the new action as CurrentAction.

```
public void SetHeroAction(HeroAction action)
{
  if (CurrentAction != action)
  {
    _model.Rotate(0, 90, 0);

    switch (action)
    {
      case HeroAction.Run:
            _model.PlayAnimation("Run", true, 0.2f);
            _model.CreateBoundingBox(100, 55, 25, new Vector3(0,
27.5f, 5));
            break;
      case HeroAction.Shield:
            _model.PlayAnimation("Shield", true, 0.2f);
            _model.CreateBoundingBox(100, 48, 25, new Vector3(0,
24.0f, 10));
            break;
      case HeroAction.Slide:
            _model.PlayAnimation("Slide", true, 0.2f);
            _model.CreateBoundingBox(100, 40, 45, new Vector3(0,
20.0f, -5));
            break;
      case HeroAction.Jump:
            _model.PlayAnimation("Jump", true, 0.2f);
            break;
```

```
    case HeroAction.Die:
        _velocity = Vector2.Zero;
        _model.Translate(_model.LocalPosition.X, Path.GROUND_
POS, _model.LocalPosition.Z);
        _model.SetAnimationSpeed(0.5f);
        _model.Rotate(0, 0, 0);
        _model.PlayAnimation("Die", false);
        break;
    }
    CurrentAction = action;
    }
}
```

Update

The `Update` method is the engine of the hero, shifting between lines of code based on the `CurrentAction` object. We start by checking if the `CurrentAction` object is equal to `HeroAction.Die`, if it is we don't want to do anything besides calling `base.Update`.

```
if (CurrentAction == HeroAction.Die)
{
    base.Update(renderContext);
    return;
}
```

It's time to implement the state machine. This system controls the hero state based on our input and some other parameters.

1. Calculate the current animation speed based on the division of `RenderContext.GameSpeed` by `RenderContext.InitialGameSpeed`.

2. Set the model's animation speed. If our `animSpeed` is `NaN` (Not a Number), we set it to `0` (division by zero results in a `NaN` float).

3. `Switch` case is based on the `CurrentAction` object.

4. In case of `HeroAction.Run`:

   ◦ We check if one of the buttons is pressed and call `SetHeroAction` with the corresponding `HeroAction`

   ◦ If the jump button is pressed, we also need to reset `_jumpTimer` and set the `_velocity.Y` to `JUMP_SPEED`

5. In case of `HeroAction.Shield` or `HeroAction.Slide`:

   ◦ We check if the corresponding button is still pressed, and if it's released, we set the hero state back to running

6. In case of `HeroAction.Jump`:

   ○ Add the `ElapsedGameTime.TotalSeconds` property to `_jumpTimer`

   ○ Decrease `_velocity.Y` by twice `JUMP_SPEED` per second

   ○ If the jump button is still pressed and `_velocity.Y` is smaller than zero (which means that the hero will descend) and the `_jumpTimer` smaller than `JUMP_TIMEOUT`, then we need to keep hovering, so we set `_velocity.Y` to 0

   ○ Else if the model's y-position is smaller than the ground level, then we know that the hero touched the ground, that is, to force the jump button release, to set the component of the `_velocity.Y` field field to `zeroReset` and the model's position to the ground level, and to set the state back to running

7. In case of `HeroAction.None`:

   ○ Set the state back to running

```
//STATE MACHINE
var animSpeed = 0.5f*(renderContext.GameSpeed/
renderContext.InitialGameSpeed);           _model.
SetAnimationSpeed(float.IsNaN(animSpeed)?0:animSpeed);

switch (CurrentAction)
{
  case HeroAction.Run:

         if (ButtonsController.SlidePressed)
         {
           SetHeroAction(HeroAction.Slide);
         }
         else if (ButtonsController.ShieldPressed)
         {
           SetHeroAction(HeroAction.Shield);
         }
         else if (ButtonsController.JumpPressed)
         {
           _jumpTimer = 0;
           SetHeroAction(HeroAction.Jump);
           _velocity.Y = JUMP_SPEED;
         }
         break;

    case HeroAction.Shield:
         if (!ButtonsController.ShieldPressed)
```

```
            SetHeroAction(HeroAction.Run);
        break;
    case HeroAction.Slide:
        if (!ButtonsController.SlidePressed)
          SetHeroAction(HeroAction.Run);
        break;
    case HeroAction.Jump:
        _jumpTimer += (float) renderContext.GameTime.
ElapsedGameTime.TotalSeconds;
        _velocity.Y -= (JUMP_SPEED*2f)*(float)
renderContext.GameTime.ElapsedGameTime.TotalSeconds;

        if ((ButtonsController.JumpPressed && _velocity.Y
< 0) && _jumpTimer < JUMP_TIMEOUT)
          _velocity.Y = 0;
        else if (_model.LocalPosition.Y <= Path.GROUND_POS)
        {
          ButtonsController.ForceButtonRelease(0);
          _velocity.Y = 0;
          _model.LocalPosition = new Vector3(_
model.LocalPosition.X, Path.GROUND_POS,
_model.LocalPosition.Z);
            SetHeroAction(HeroAction.Run);
        }
        break;
    case HeroAction.None:
        SetHeroAction(HeroAction.Run);
        break;
}
```

The last thing we need to do is updating the hero's position. We set _velocity.X to the current game speed and calculate the new position based on the velocity.

```
//POSITION
_velocity.X = renderContext.GameSpeed;
var newPos = _model.LocalPosition + (new Vector3(_
velocity, 0)*(float)renderContext.GameTime.
ElapsedGameTime.TotalSeconds);
_model.Translate(newPos);.
base.Update(renderContext);
```

Scene implementation

Our `Hero` class is ready and can be implemented in the `LevelScene` class. First of all, we need to add a new field in the `LevelScene` class.

```
private Hero _hero;
```

In the `Initialize` method of `LevelScene`, we will initialize and position our object and add it to the scene.

```
_hero = new Hero();
_hero.Translate(-100, 0, 0);
AddSceneObject(_hero);
```

We also need to initialize the `RenderContext.InitialGameSpeed` property.

```
SceneManager.RenderContext.GameSpeed =
SceneManager.RenderContext.InitialGameSpeed = 100;
```

When we run the game and press `Start`, we can see our hero running on the path. When we press one of the buttons, the hero plays another animation and the bounding box changes.

Swing Ball

This is one of the obstacles that our hero must evade by sliding under it. We will attach a bounding box to the swinging ball itself, but before we can do that, we need to create an empty object that contains our bounding box. This way we can attach the bounding box to the ball itself because that's the only part that collides with the hero. The next screenshot gives us a better understanding of the bounding box setup.

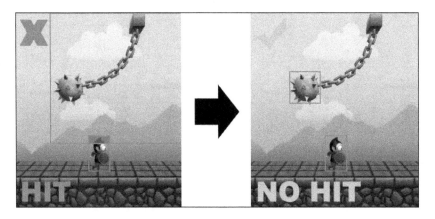

Prerequisites

We need an object that contains our bounding box, GameObject3D, but because this class is abstract, we can't create an instance from it. That is why we need to create a new object that inherits from GameObject3D. Create a new class called EmptyObject3D that inherits from GameObject3D.

```
public class EmptyObject3D : GameObject3D
```

That's all we need to do for this class. Now we can start building the swinging ball class. Create a class called SwingBall that inherits from GameObject3D.

```
public class SwingBall : GameObject3D
```

Fields

The only fields we need are GameAnimatedModel and EmptyObject3D for its bounding box.

```
private GameAnimatedModel _model;
private EmptyObject3D _ballHitregion;
```

Initialize

In the initialize method, we initialize, position, scale, and add _model. We also initialize and add _ballHitRegion. Because _ballHitRegion contains the bounding box of the ball, we need to create a bounding box for that object. We draw the bounding box for debugging purposes.

```
_model = new GameAnimatedModel("Models\\SwingBall");
_model.Translate(0,242,-100);
_model.Scale(new Vector3(0.76f));
AddChild(_model);

_ballHitregion = new EmptyObject3D();
_ballHitregion.CreateBoundingBox(90,90,100);
_ballHitregion.DrawBoundingBox = true;
AddChild(_ballHitregion);
```

LoadContent

We can only set the animation after the model is loaded because it's only then that the animation data is available.

```
base.LoadContent(contentManager);
_model.PlayAnimation("Swing");
_model.SetAnimationSpeed(0.8f);
```

Update

In the `Update` method we extract the bone matrix called `BallBone` from the ball; this matrix contains the position for the bounding box. But we always want the latest position, so we need to update the model before extracting the bone matrix of the ball. And because we set the new `_ballHitregion` after the `base.Update` we have to call it manually.

```
base.Update(renderContext);

var boneMat = _model.GetBoneTransform("BallBone");
_ballHitregion.Translate(boneMat.Translation - LocalPosition);
_ballHitregion.Update(renderContext);
```

Scene implementation

This implementation is temporary, because after we made all the obstacles, we will put them in an array. But we can create a `SwingBall` now for testing purpose. First of all we need to add a new field in the `LevelScene` class.

```
private SwingBall _testBall;
```

In the `Initialize` method of `LevelScene`, we will initialize our object and add it to the scene.

```
_testBall = new SwingBall();
AddSceneObject(_testBall);
```

Change the game speed from 100 to 0; this way the camera won't move and our `_testBall` stays in the viewing area. The hero animations won't work if the game speed is zero. Don't forget to reset it afterwards. When we run the game and press **Start**, we can see our ball swinging. Note that the bounding box is following the ball's position, as shown in the following screenshot:

Spikes

The second obstacle one can be avoided by jumping over it. Create a class called
Spikes that inherits from GameObject3D.

```
public class Spikes : GameObject3D
```

Fields

This object has one field, that is, Model.

```
private GameModel _model;
```

Initialize

In the Initialize method, we initialize, position, scale, and add _model.
We also need a bounding box and set the DrawBoundingBox property to
true for debugging purposes.

```
_model = new GameModel("Models\\Spikes");
_model.CreateBoundingBox(30,20,30, new Vector3(0,10,0));
_model.Translate(0,Path.GROUND_POS,-100);
_model.Scale(new Vector3(1.5f));
_model.DrawBoundingBox = true;
AddChild(_model);
```

Scene implementation

Same as with the SwingBall class, we create a temporary _testSprikes object
for testing purposes. The implementation is also the same as the _testBall
implementation, except for the type of the object. When we run the game and press
Start, we can see some spikes on the path, as shown in the following screenshot:

Enemy

Our third and last obstacle is the rock-throwing enemy. This enemy is similar to the enemy we used in previous chapters. But for the game, we need to improve it a bit. Create a class called Enemy that inherits from GameObject3D.

Fields and properties

The Enemy class has multiple fields; _enemyModel, _rockModel, some variables to control the drop, and an explosion sprite sheet. We also need the world position of the hero, and that's why we also have a field of type Hero.

```
private GameAnimatedModel _enemyModel;

private GameModel _rockModel;
private bool _rockFalling;
private Vector3 _rockDirection;
public bool RockHit { get; set; }
private float _rockSpeed;

private GameAnimatedSprite _explosionSprite;
private Hero _hero;
```

Constructor

The constructor is fairly simple. It has one argument of type Hero and inside the constructor, we assign this argument to our _hero field.

```
public Enemy(Hero hero)
{
_hero = hero;
}
```

Initialize

It is time to initialize and add all the objects. Note that we don't add _explosionSprite because it's of type GameObject2D. Thus, we need to call its methods manually. The bounding box is assigned to _rockModel, because that's the object that hits us.

```
_enemyModel = new GameAnimatedModel("Models\\Enemy");
_enemyModel.AnimationComplete += EnemyAnimationComplete;
_enemyModel.Translate(0,150,-100);
AddChild(_enemyModel);
```

```
_rockModel = new GameModel("Models\\Rock");
_rockModel.CreateBoundingBox(30,30,30);
_rockModel.DrawBoundingBox = true;
AddChild(_rockModel);

_explosionSprite = new GameAnimatedSprite("Sprites\\Explosion_
Spritesheet", 16, 50, new Point(64, 64), 4);
_explosionSprite.Scale(new Vector2(2f));
_explosionSprite.Initialize();
```

EnemyAnimationComplete method

When the enemy's drop animation is completed, we change it back to the
fly animation.

```
private void EnemyAnimationComplete(string name)
{
    if(name.Equals("Drop"))
        _enemyModel.PlayAnimation("Fly",true,0.2f);
}
```

LoadContent

We need to call the `LoadContent` method of `_explosionSprite` manually and also
start the fly animation of our enemy model. Note that we call everything after calling
`base.LoadContent`.

```
base.LoadContent(contentManager);
_explosionSprite.LoadContent(contentManager);
_enemyModel.PlayAnimation("Fly");
```

Update

The `Update` method is pretty straight forward. The following steps explain most
of the code and logic:

1. If the rock is falling and didn't hit anything, we update its position based
   on `_rockDirection` and `_rockSpeed`. If the y-position of the rock is smaller
   than or equal to the ground level, then we set `RockHit` to `true`.

2. If the rock is falling but `RockHit` is `true`, meaning that the rock has hit
   something, then we project the rock's position to a two-dimensional
   coordinate and play the explosion at that position. When the explosion is
   finished, we need to reset some of the states.

3. When the rock is not falling, meaning that the enemy holds it, we can calculate the rock's position based on the `Rock_Position` bone matrix of the enemy. Note that we do these calculations again after calling `base.Update`. If distance between the hero and the enemy is smaller than a certain amount, we can drop the rock. We calculate the speed and direction of the rock based on the hero's future position (the position after 1 second, so we just add game speed to the hero's world position). Setting `_rockFalling` to `true` restarts the code from step 1.

```
if (_rockFalling)
{
  if (!RockHit)
  {
    var rockPos = _rockModel.LocalPosition;
    rockPos -= _rockDirection*_rockSpeed*(float) renderContext.
GameTime.ElapsedGameTime.TotalSeconds;
    _rockModel.Translate(rockPos);

    if (rockPos.Y <= Path.GROUND_POS)
    {
      RockHit = true;
    }
  }
  else
  {
    _rockModel.CanDraw = false;

    var projVec = renderContext.GraphicsDevice.Viewport.
Project(_rockModel.WorldPosition, renderContext.Camera.Projection,
renderContext.Camera.View, Matrix.Identity);

    _explosionSprite.Translate(new Vector2(projVec.X - 64,
projVec.Y - 64));
    _explosionSprite.PlayAnimation();
    _explosionSprite.Update(renderContext);

    if (!_explosionSprite.IsPlaying)
    {
      _rockModel.CanDraw = true;
      _rockFalling = false;
      RockHit = false;
    }
  }
}
```

```
    base.Update(renderContext);

    if(!_rockFalling)
    {
      var boneMat = _enemyModel.GetBoneTransform("Rock_Position");
      _rockModel.Translate(boneMat.Translation - LocalPosition);
      _rockModel.Update(renderContext);

      var heroDistance = WorldPosition.X - _hero.WorldPos.X;
      if(Math.Abs(heroDistance) <= 250)
      {
        var futureHeroHitPos = _hero.WorldPos + new
Vector3(renderContext.GameSpeed, 60, 0);
        _rockDirection = _rockModel.WorldPosition - futureHeroHitPos;
        _rockSpeed = _rockDirection.Length();
        _rockDirection.Normalize();
        _enemyModel.PlayAnimation("Drop",false,0.5f);
        _rockFalling = true;
      }
    }
```

Draw

We need to call the `_explosionSprite.Draw` method manually when the rock hits something. Note that we also need to call the `SpriteBatch.Begin/End` methods because we are currently in the three-dimensional draw loop. We also need to reset some of the `Renderstate` properties afterwards.

```
  if(RockHit)
  {
    renderContext.SpriteBatch.Begin();
    _explosionSprite.Draw(renderContext);
    renderContext.SpriteBatch.End();

    //Reset Renderstate
    renderContext.GraphicsDevice.BlendState = BlendState.Opaque;
    renderContext.GraphicsDevice.DepthStencilState = DepthStencilState.
Default;
    renderContext.GraphicsDevice.SamplerStates[0] = SamplerState.
LinearWrap;
  }
```

Scene implementation

Same as with the spikes, we create a temporary _testEnemy object for testing purposes. The implementation is also the same as the _testEnemy implementation, except for the type of the object. When we run the game and press **Start**, we can see the enemy flying and throwing rocks at you, but at the moment, they only collide with the path.

Perspective Camera

Up to now, we've always used an orthogonal camera projection, but we can enhance the three-dimensional feeling by adding a perspective projection. The changes are very simple and similar to the orthogonal camera; it's only the projection matrix that needs to change. Create a new class called PerspectiveCamera that inherits from BaseCamera.

```
public class PerspectiveCamera: BaseCamera
```

Constructor

To achieve a perspective projection, we need to change the projection matrix. We can use the Matrix.CreatePerspectiveFieldOfView method to create a perspective projection matrix. The arguments are: the field of view in radians, the aspect ratio (screen width/screen height), near clipping plane, and the far clipping plane.

```
Projection = Matrix.CreatePerspectiveFieldOfView((float)Math.PI /
3.0f, 800f / 480f, 0.1f, 700);
```

Bringing it all together

It's time to build our game using all the objects we've made and stick everything together in the LevelScene class. These are the things we still need to do:

- Create an obstacle spawn system
- Handle collisions between hero and obstacles
- Add a game over state
- Add the perspective camera
- Add some background music

Extra fields

The LevelScene class already contains some fields but we need to add some more.

- A GameSprite object that contains the game over sign
- A list of GameObject3D that contains all the obstacles
- An obstacle threshold, indicating when we want to place a new obstacle
- A float datatype that keeps our total move amount from the last obstacle
- A integer datatype that counts the amount of obstacles we've passed

```
private GameSprite _gameOverSprite;
private List<GameObject3D> _obstacles = new List<GameObject3D>();
private const float SET_OBSTACLE_THRESHOLD = 700;
private float _moveAmount;
private int _speedUpCount;
```

Don't forget to delete the test obstacle objects.

AddObstacle method

We will create a method that makes it easy to add new obstacles to the list. Inside this method, we will add the obstacle to the LevelScene class and obstacle list.

```
private void AddObstacle(GameObject3D obstacle)
{
  AddSceneObject(obstacle);
  _obstacles.Add(obstacle);
}
```

ResetLevel method

This method will reset some fields to their initial state. This way we can start the game again from the beginning. The following steps explain the reset process:

1. Translate all the obstacles back to a position behind the hero and out of the view area.

2. Reset the hero action to None using the SetHeroAction method.

3. Reset the GameSpeed property and InitialGameSpeed back to its initial value.

4. Stop drawing the game over sign and draw the trigger buttons.

5. Reset _moveAmount en _SpeedUpCount back to 0.

```
private void ResetLevel()
{
    _obstacles.ForEach(obstacle => obstacle.Translate(-1000, 0, 0));
    _hero.SetHeroAction(Hero.HeroAction.None);

    SceneManager.RenderContext.GameSpeed =
    SceneManager.RenderContext.InitialGameSpeed = 100;

    _gameOverSprite.CanDraw = false;
    _buttonsController.CanDraw = true;

    _moveAmount = 0;
    _speedUpCount = 0;
}
```

Deactivate

This is one of the virtual methods of GameScene. Each time we go to another scene, we want to reset the level.

```
public override void Deactivated()
{
    ResetLevel();
    base.Deactivated();
}
```

SetObstacle method

Each time we want to place another obstacle, we will call this method. This method randomly selects one of the obstacles from the list and positions it in front of the hero. It will only do that if the chosen obstacle is far behind the player. The position is set based on the current camera's x-position that we retrieve from the method's argument. We do a maximum of 10 iterations to prevent endless looping.

```
private void SetObstacle(Vector3 camPos)
{
  var currentIteration = 0;
  while(true)
  {
    if (currentIteration >= 10) break;

    var randomIndex = new Random().Next(0, _obstacles.Count);

    if (_obstacles[randomIndex].WorldPosition.X < (camPos.X - SET_
OBSTACLE_THRESHOLD))
    {
      _obstacles[randomIndex].Translate(new Vector3(camPos.X + SET_
OBSTACLE_THRESHOLD, 0, 0));
      break;
    }

    ++currentIteration;
  }
}
```

Initialize extension

There are still some objects that need to be initialized and added to the `LevelScene` class. We need to add the game over sign, the obstacles, and the perspective camera. If every object is initialized (after calling `base.Initialize`), we call the `ResetLevel` method to ensure that every object has the correct state.

```
_gameOverSprite = new GameSprite("Sprites\\GameOver");
_gameOverSprite.Translate(140,180);
AddSceneObject(_gameOverSprite);

AddObstacle(new SwingBall());
AddObstacle(new SwingBall());
AddObstacle(new Spikes());
AddObstacle(new Spikes());
AddObstacle(new Enemy());
AddObstacle(new Enemy());

var cam = new PerspectiveCamera();
cam.Rotate(-5,0,0);
cam.Translate(0,50,350);
```

```
SceneManager.RenderContext.Camera = cam;
AddSceneObject(SceneManager.RenderContext.Camera);

base.Initialize();

ResetLevel();
```

Update extension

Time to add all the game logic to the LevelScene class. The following steps explain the update logic:

1. We check if the current hero action is equal to HeroAction.Die, if it is then we've reached the game over state. Setting the GameSpeed property to zero will freeze all the objects. We hide the button triggers and show the game over sign. We switch to the menu screen if the player pressed somewhere on the screen. This gives the player the chance to restart the game.

2. If the hero is still alive, then we perform a normal update.

3. By checking the collisions:
   - We iterate the obstacle list and perform a hit test with the hero.
   - If there is a hit and the obstacle isn't an enemy, then we set the hero action to HeroAction.Die.
   - If there is a hit and the obstacle is an enemy, then we tell the enemy that its rock can explode. If the current hero action isn't equal to HeroAction.Shield, then we know that the hero must die, so we set the hero action to HeroAction.Die.

4. Move the camera; this code was added previously.

5. Set a new obstacle
   - Each frame we add the movement to _moveAmount.
   - If _moveAmount is bigger than or equal to the threshold, we can set a new obstacle by calling the SetObstacle method. We also need to reset _moveAmount.
   - Increase _speedUpCount and when this value is bigger than or equal to five, we will increase the GameSpeed property by 30 until it reached a value of 300

     ```
     if (_hero.CurrentAction == Hero.HeroAction.Die)
     {
       //GAME OVER!
       renderContext.GameSpeed = 0;
     ```

```
  _buttonsController.CanDraw = false;
  _gameOverSprite.CanDraw = true;

  if (renderContext.TouchPanelState.Count > 0
&& renderContext.TouchPanelState[0].State ==
TouchLocationState.Released)
  {
      SceneManager.SetActiveScene("Menu");
  }
}
else
{
  //OBSTACLE COLLISION
  foreach (var obstacle in _obstacles)
  {
    if (_hero.HitTest(obstacle))
    {
      if (obstacle is Enemy)
      {
        (obstacle as Enemy).RockHit = true;

        if (_hero.CurrentAction != Hero.HeroAction.
Shield)
          _hero.SetHeroAction(Hero.HeroAction.Die);
      }
      else
      {
        _hero.SetHeroAction(Hero.HeroAction.Die);
      }
    }
  }

  //CAMERA MOVEMENT
  var camPos = renderContext.Camera.LocalPosition;
  camPos += new Vector3(renderContext.GameSpeed
* (float)renderContext.GameTime.ElapsedGameTime.
TotalSeconds, 0, 0);
  renderContext.Camera.Translate(camPos);

  //SET NEW OBSTACLE
  _moveAmount += renderContext.GameSpeed * (float)
renderContext.GameTime.ElapsedGameTime.TotalSeconds;
  if (_moveAmount >= SET_OBSTACLE_THRESHOLD)
  {
    _moveAmount = 0;
```

```
            SetObstacle(camPos);

            ++_speedUpCount;
            if (_speedUpCount >= 5)
            {
              _speedUpCount = 0;
              renderContext.GameSpeed += 30;
              if (renderContext.GameSpeed > 300)
                 renderContext.GameSpeed = 300;
            }
        }
    }
```

It's also a good thing to set the DrawBoundingBox property of the different objects to false. And our game is finally ready! Have fun playing your first self-made mobile game!

Summary

In this chapter, we've built a game using a basic framework. We've seen how different game mechanics can work together to create a simple and interesting game.

It's always more fun if you're able to share your game with the world. In the next chapter, we will see how to release a game on the Windows Phone Store!

8
Releasing our game

Up until now, we've gained all the technical knowledge we need to develop games for Windows Phone. Unfortunately, that's not all the knowledge we need. If we want to release our game, we need to test it thoroughly and follow some rules before submitting it to the marketplace. After that, our game needs to pass validation before it is released to the Windows Phone Marketplace. Note that there is no way to share our game with friends without the Marketplace, unless their phone is unlocked.

In this chapter we will cover:

- Testing our game
- Creating a trial version of our game
- Application certification requirements
- Application submission process

Testing

Before submitting your application to the Windows Phone Marketplace, we need to make sure it is bug-free. Therefore we need to test it thoroughly. This quote from Rich Cook says it all:

> *Programmers are in a race with the Universe to create bigger and better idiot-proof programs, while the Universe is trying to create bigger and better idiots. So far the Universe is winning.*

So when we test our game, we have to make sure it is done thoroughly. This means testing everything a user might do and running against every possible wall. Don't do this alone, but let other people who don't know our game test it.

Another thing is try to write a unit test as we are developing. A unit test is a test which tests a specific piece of code. A good framework for this is NUnit. More information about unit tests can be found on `http://www.nunit.org/`.

Creating a trial version

When we release a game to the Windows Phone Marketplace, it is good to provide a trial version of our game. XNA offers functionality for easily creating trial and full games. We can use the following code to see if our game is a trial:

```
Guide.IsTrialMode
```

Note that, unlike on Xbox 360, the phone has no system-side imposition of limits; this is completely up to the developer. More information and best practices about creating trial applications can be found at `http://msdn.microsoft.com/en-us/library/ff967558(v=vs.92).aspx`.

Application certification requirements

When we submit an application, it has to pass certification. The goal of this certification is to make sure our application is reliable, uses resources efficiently, doesn't interfere with the phone's functionality and does not contain viruses of other malicious software. Therefore we must follow certain rules. These rules range from the fact that the user must be able to receive calls when gaming (and we must thus suspend the game) to the fact that we can't suspend the players music without asking for permission. The set of rules covers six categories:

- Application certification requirements for Windows Phone
- Application policies
- Content policies
- Application submission requirements
- Technical certification requirements
- Additional requirements for Specific Application Types

If and only if our application passes all tests, can it be released to the Windows Phone Marketplace. Because these rules might change from time to time, we will not put them in this book. Instead, a detailed list of the rules can be found at `http://msdn.microsoft.com/en-us/library/hh184843(v=VS.92).aspx`.

Application submission process

If we are confident that our game will pass all certification, we can go ahead and submit it. First of all we must have a valid Dev Center subscription. This costs $99 per year, and *Chapter 1, Getting Started*, describes how we can get one. If we have a valid subscription, we can submit our games via the Dev Center dashboard. This means uploading the XAP file that we can find at [project path] /Bin/Release to the Dev Center Dashboard. Uploading is done in the following steps:

1. Uploading our game and specifying a name and a version, along with several screenshots of the game.
2. Describing our game.
3. Determining price.
4. Providing optional testing instructions.
5. Submitting.

A detailed walkthrough of the submission process can be found at http://msdn. microsoft.com/en-us/library/windowsphone/help/jj206724(v=vs.105).aspx.

Summary

In this chapter, we've covered what we still need to do if we want to release our game. This includes some formalities that have to be fulfilled and some administration. This is however incredibly important, because if we don't follow them exactly, our game will not pass certification and thus won't be released.

Index

T

touch
used, for user input 64, 65
TouchCollection 65

U

unit test 132
UnloadContent method, Game class 15
Update method, Game class 15
Update method, GameObject2D 24
user input, handling
accelerometer, using 63
gestures, using 65
keyboard, using 61
touch, using 64

W

Windows Phone
application, creating 10
application, deploying 10
developing 7
registering 9, 10
Windows Phone application
creating 10, 11
deploying 12
Windows Phone Marketplace
game, releasing 132
Windows Phone SDK
installing 8

X

XACT 69
XNA Game Studio
about 12
Game class 13

About Packt Publishing

Packt, pronounced 'packed', published its first book "Mastering phpMyAdmin for Effective MySQL Management" in April 2004 and subsequently continued to specialize in publishing highly focused books on specific technologies and solutions.

Our books and publications share the experiences of your fellow IT professionals in adapting and customizing today's systems, applications, and frameworks. Our solution based books give you the knowledge and power to customize the software and technologies you're using to get the job done. Packt books are more specific and less general than the IT books you have seen in the past. Our unique business model allows us to bring you more focused information, giving you more of what you need to know, and less of what you don't.

Packt is a modern, yet unique publishing company, which focuses on producing quality, cutting-edge books for communities of developers, administrators, and newbies alike. For more information, please visit our website: www.packtpub.com.

About Packt Enterprise

In 2010, Packt launched two new brands, Packt Enterprise and Packt Open Source, in order to continue its focus on specialization. This book is part of the Packt Enterprise brand, home to books published on enterprise software – software created by major vendors, including (but not limited to) IBM, Microsoft and Oracle, often for use in other corporations. Its titles will offer information relevant to a range of users of this software, including administrators, developers, architects, and end users.

Writing for Packt

We welcome all inquiries from people who are interested in authoring. Book proposals should be sent to author@packtpub.com. If your book idea is still at an early stage and you would like to discuss it first before writing a formal book proposal, contact us; one of our commissioning editors will get in touch with you.

We're not just looking for published authors; if you have strong technical skills but no writing experience, our experienced editors can help you develop a writing career, or simply get some additional reward for your expertise.

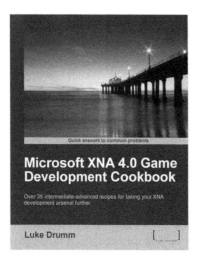

Microsoft XNA 4.0 Game Development Cookbook

ISBN: 978-1-849691-98-7   Paperback: 356 pages

Over 35 intermediate-advanced recipes for taking your XNA development arsenal further

1. Accelerate your XNA learning with a myriad of tips and tricks to solve your everyday problems

2. Get to grips with adding special effects, virtual atmospheres and computer controlled characters with this book and e-book

3. A fast-paced cookbook packed with screenshots to illustrate each advanced step by step task

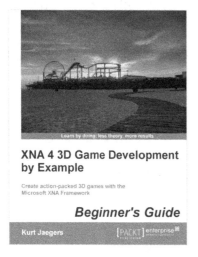

XNA 4 3D Game Development by Example: Beginner's Guide

ISBN: 978-1-849687-08-9   Paperback: 322 pages

Create action-packed 3D games with the Microsoft XNA Framework

1. Learn the structure of a 3D world and how to implement a variety of 3D techniques including terrain generation and 3D model rendering.

2. Build three different types of 3D games step-by-step, including a first-person maze game, a battlefield tank game, and a 3D sidescrolling action game on the surface of Mars.

3. Learn to utilize High Level Shader Language (HLSL) to add lighting and multi-texturing effects to your 3D scenes.

Please check **www.PacktPub.com** for information on our titles

Windows Phone 7 XNA Cookbook

ISBN: 978-1-849691-20-8   Paperback: 450 pages

Over 70 recipes for making your own Windows Phone 7 game

1. Complete focus on the best Windows Phone 7 game development techniques using XNA 4.0

2. Easy to follow cookbook allowing you to dive in wherever you want.

3. Convert ideas into action using practical recipes

XNA 4.0 Game Development by Example – Visual Basic Edition

ISBN: 978-1-849692-40-3   Paperback: 424 pages

Create your own exciting games with Visual Basic and Microsoft XNA 4.0

1. Visual Basic edition of Kurt Jaegers' XNA 4.0 Game Development by Example. The first book to target Visual Basic developers who want to develop games with the XNA framework

2. Dive headfirst into game creation with Visual Basic and the XNA Framework

3. Four different styles of games comprising a puzzler, space shooter, multi-axis shoot 'em up, and a jump-and-run platformer

Please check **www.PacktPub.com** for information on our titles

www.ingramcontent.com/pod-product-compliance
Lightning Source LLC
LaVergne TN
LVHW062318060326
832902LV00013B/2296